W9-BHV-316

WITH COMPLIMENTS OF
J.C. FLOWERS & CO. LLC

THE FINANCIAL CRISIS

THE FINANCIAL CRISIS

Who is to Blame?

Howard Davies

polity

The right of Howard Davies to be identified as Author of this Work has been asserted in accordance with the UK Copyright, Designs and Patents Act 1988.

First published in 2010 by Polity Press

Polity Press
65 Bridge Street
Cambridge CB2 1UR, UK

Polity Press
350 Main Street
Malden, MA 02148, USA

ISBN-13: 978-0-7456-5163-7 (hardback)
ISBN-13: 978-0-7456-5164-4 (paperback))

A catalogue record for this book is available from the British Library.

Typeset in 11 on 13 pt Palatino
by Servis Filmsetting Ltd, Stockport, Cheshire
Printed and bound in Great Britain by MPG Books Group Limited, Bodmin, Cornwall

The publisher has used its best endeavours to ensure that the URLs for external websites referred to in this book are correct and active at the time of going to press. However, the publisher has no responsibility for the websites and can make no guarantee that a site will remain live or that the content is or will remain appropriate.

Every effort has been made to trace all copyright holders, but if any have been inadvertently overlooked the publisher will be pleased to include any necessary credits in any subsequent reprint or edition.

For further information on Polity, visit our website: www.politybooks.com

CONTENTS

ACKNOWLEDGEMENTS

In preparing this guide I have benefited from discussions with politicians, central bankers, regulators and market participants. Some of them are quoted in the relevant sections; others are not.

I am particularly grateful to Stephanie Morisset for her help in preparing the text and the references, with ready support from Veronique Mizgailo, Kaylee Stewart and Jagoda Sumicka.

INTRODUCTION

The crisis which engulfed the world, beginning in 2007, was the most destructive economic event of the last eighty years.

Triggered by problems in the United States' subprime mortgage market in the summer of 2007, it soon spread to other related and unrelated financial markets and then into the real economy. The global economy, which had grown by 3.5 per cent per year on average over the previous decade, contracted by over 1 per cent in 2009, with far sharper falls in the advanced industrialized countries. Peak to trough reductions in GDP were around 6 per cent in the main developed economies. By late 2009, growth had begun to recover in some of them, though not all. But the economic costs will continue to be felt for some time. Global unemployment is estimated to be 15 million higher than it was before the crisis. There has been an enormous loss of value in the financial sector also, with estimates suggesting that financial firms will need recapitalization totalling $16.0 trillion.

Governments were successful, as they had not been in the 1930s, in using fiscal policy to prevent the world sliding into a full-scale depression. Fiscal stabilizers were allowed to operate, and in many places direct stimuli were introduced. These initiatives were effective, up to a point, but the costs in terms of government deficits and an increase in the stock of government debt have been enormous. The total debt outstanding of major Western economies is expected to rise from 84.1 per cent of GDP in 2007 to 109.9 per cent in 2010, with a number of countries showing debt to GDP ratios well above 100 per cent. These debts will be a serious drag on the economies of the affected countries for many years to come. Future generations will be paying for this crisis for decades.

It is therefore not surprising that there has been a massive outpouring of analysis and commentary, designed to identify the causes of the crisis and the appropriate remedies to reduce the risk of a recurrence. Some of this analysis has become personal – commentators have asked not simply what was to blame for the crisis, but who. The old saying has it that success has a hundred fathers, but failure is an orphan. In this case, that has been turned on its head. As time passed, explanations proliferated and the list of guilty men (and a few women) continued to lengthen. Far from opinion converging on one explanation of the crisis, views tended to diverge, with a range of competing narratives articulated.

A common element was the identification of excess leverage as the key underlying problem. But why was that leverage allowed to develop? Whose leverage was most important in contributing to the crash? And what should be done to prevent the same thing happening again in the future?

One narrative identified a series of macroeconomic trends which led to an unsustainable global economy, which was bound to unwind sooner or later. Massive global imbalances were allowed to build up in the early years of this century, with huge current account surpluses in China and the oil-producing countries, matched by enormous deficits in the US, the UK, and elsewhere. These imbalances created a surplus of liquidity – a savings glut – which went in search of apparently safe assets generating a higher return than government debt. This process was facilitated, indeed positively encouraged, by loose monetary policy in the United States following the dot-com boom and bust and the Twin Towers attack. So, on this analysis, bad macroeconomic policy was the number one culprit.

But why did these imbalances build up? Some argue that China, with its export-led growth model, was the most important contributor. Others prefer to see the fault on the

US side. American consumers had become used to levels of consumption, and a standard of living, higher than their income could justify. Why blame the Chinese for feeding this insidious habit?

Still others look behind these global trends and identify growing income inequalities, especially in the United States, as a key factor. While the top deciles of the income distribution were doing well, middle- and lower-income American households were unable to maintain their previous standard of living, or certainly to maintain a rising standard, and used growing indebtedness as an attempt to compensate for falling real incomes. This growing income inequality was reinforced by the Bush administration's tax policy which further biased the rewards of growth towards the better off.

An alternative strand of thinking, which also sees government policy as a crucial contributory factor, puts the argument very differently. Successive US administrations sought to encourage increasing levels of home ownership, for political reasons. That could only be achieved by making debt available to less creditworthy households. That, in turn, required government intervention in the market through legislation – the Community Reinvestment Act – and through the two government-supported entities, Fannie Mae and Freddie Mac, who guaranteed subprime mortgages. So it was too much government, intervening in financial markets to achieve a certain social outcome, which eventually destabilized the economy.

But there is a strongly held rival view, which suggests a very different role for government in the build-up to the crisis. Governments in the United States and the United Kingdom, in particular, had encouraged the growth of the financial sector, and the growth of financial innovation, by a series of deregulatory measures over a long period. So it was too little, not too much government that was the problem. Congress, in particular, was heavily influenced by costly lobbying by Wall Street firms. Had governments kept a tighter rein on financial markets and financial institutions, then the outcome would have been very different.

Many politicians acknowledge the possibility that macro-economic conditions may have been a contributory factor, but understandably prefer arguments based on the behaviour of the financial sector. Even governments, like those in Washington and London, which had traditionally maintained close links with financial firms and their leaders, began to adopt a very different style of rhetoric about them as the crisis developed. A narrative which identified fundamental flaws in the operation of financial markets began to be developed. On this argument, it was undisciplined market behaviour which lay at the heart of the financial instability which erupted so damagingly in 2007. Exotic financial innovations, whose social utility was doubtful, were driven by incentive structures which rewarded market participants extravagantly, sometimes for short-term returns which left their firms dangerously exposed to potential longer-term losses.

For some time, earnings in the financial sector had been outpacing those in other parts of the economy. These trends were tolerated, perhaps even encouraged, by politicians who looked to wealthy financiers for support, whether for their own election campaigns or for favoured projects in the arts and charities. Those high earnings began to look very different in the light of the crisis. How was it that a small number of individuals could have extracted such high rents from their position in the markets? In particular, after almost all major financial institutions had to be rescued by governments in late 2008, how could it be that individuals could earn huge bonuses in one year, when losses in the following year were 'socialized' and in effect underwritten by taxpayers? It was argued that we had allowed a situation to develop in which there was a fundamental asymmetry – heads the financial firms won, tails the taxpayer lost.

This became a widely held view about the financial sector generally. But some specific villains were identified, too, whose actions were thought to have contributed significantly to the problems with which governments were wrestling. Unregulated hedge funds and private equity firms were highlighted. Credit rating agencies, whose actions had undoubtedly been a part of the subprime bubble problem, were similarly seen as institutions with a strong case to answer and to be riddled with conflicts of interest and dangerous perverse incentives. Among the investment banks, Goldman Sachs became the favoured target.

And what of the institutions put in place to regulate these markets? Another strand of argument identified their failings as being central to the problem. Auditors facilitated accounting tricks which concealed leverage. Regulators had the power to require banks to hold more capital and larger reserves, yet did not use them. They allowed new instruments of speculation to be introduced, without adequate risk management controls around them. To these general criticisms were added some specifics – the Federal Reserve could have had some regulated mortgage lending but chose not to do so, for example. In the UK, the structure of regulation put in place by the Labour government after 1997 was seen to have misfired, especially at the beginning of the crisis in 2007.

Why did regulators maintain a weak, hands-off approach? They were influenced by economists and financial theorists who had developed a set of flawed theories about efficient markets. But the field is not left to economists, politicians and regulators. Others advanced more fundamental societal explanations for the instabilities. Religious leaders entered the fray with homilies on human wickedness and greed.

It is perhaps not surprising that such a plethora of explanations should have been articulated. We are all influenced by our perceptions, prejudices and interests. Central bankers are not likely to volunteer that weak monetary policy was at the heart of the problem. Alan Greenspan's celebrated apology was very limited in its scope and did not speak to the monetary policy decisions which he himself had made. Politicians are not likely to say that they were guilty of fuelling the fire with ill-considered social interventions. Regulators rarely confess to having been asleep at the wheel. Bankers are unlikely to put their hands up and acknowledge that it was their short-term greed and recklessness which was to blame.

But there is a problem in simply observing that a wide range of explanations have been advanced. The problem is that policy responses are being proposed, and even implemented, based on narratives which may not be well supported by the evidence. Some policy changes have perhaps been advanced in the category of 'it is important never to waste a good crisis'. The measures taken to constrain offshore centres, for example, one of the least plausible sets of potential culprits, reflect the desire some Western politicians have had for some time to close off tax loopholes.

It may not matter much that the crisis allowed that to happen, but in other cases, policies implemented on the back of flawed and very partial analysis may be damaging. There is a risk that measures taken will impose long-term costs on the economy for little ultimate gain. There is also a risk that we convince ourselves that the problem has been solved through the implementation of tighter regulations here or there, and ignore some of the more difficult underlying issues.

The aim of this short book is to survey these different explanations, which are sometimes complementary, but sometimes conflicting. Thirty-eight strands are identified. In each case, the charge sheet is summarized and some of the key protagonists who have advanced the argument are identified. I briefly describe the facts that may be deduced to support the argument, and the counterarguments where there are specific points to make. There is a short list of references in each case, which allows the reader to go further. Finally, as the 39th step, there is a short consolidated assessment of the arguments which seem to me to be the most persuasive. Readers may disagree, and I acknowledge that other combinations of causes could plausibly be put together.

The book was originally devised as an aid to teaching an LSE course module on the financial crisis and the responses to it. I hope it may be useful in other similar teaching contexts, and to the general reader also. Since the economic and social costs of the crisis will be with us for some time, the debate on its origins, and the appropriate responses to them, undoubtedly still has some road to travel.

A   THE BIG PICTURE

The first four explanations focus on the political and economic background. They divide into two pairs, the first largely political, the second macroeconomic.

Does the crisis reveal fundamental flaws in the particular version of laissez-faire capitalism operated in the US and the UK in recent years? Is it the end of the line for the Reagan-Thatcher model? (Section 1)

What drove the rapid growth in borrowing – and can that be attributed to the growing income inequality which has been a feature of the last two decades? (2)

Were there features of the global macroeconomic background which generated instability, in particular the growing surplus in China and the oil-producing nations, which were reinvested in the West, driving down return on risky assets? (3) Should monetary policy have done more to offset these pressures, and to tighten financial conditions as asset prices boomed? (4)

I

FRANKENSTEIN'S MONSTER: THE END OF LAISSEZ-FAIRE CAPITALISM

Most of the arguments in this book relate to features of the management of the global economy and the international financial system which have been identified as key contributors to the crisis. But there is a broader political context. There are many who have seen the crisis as more than a 'Minsky moment' (Section 5) or a 100-year flood, and rather as a sign that the capitalist system is fundamentally flawed. There has been something of a revival of far left groups (and also of far right parties exploiting populist discontent). Marxist economic historians see the crisis as grist to their particular mill. Billy Bragg, the genial singer-songwriter and political activist, sees the crisis as a vindication of popular resistance to Thatcherite free market dogma: 'like Frankenstein's monster, Thatcherism has turned on its creators'.[1]

In using this rhetoric, Bragg finds himself quite close to mainstream opinion among centrist continental European politicians. President Sarkozy of France told supporters in 2008 that 'the idea of the all powerful market that must not be constrained by any rules, by any political intervention, was mad . . . the present crisis must incite us to refound capitalism on the basis of ethics and work . . . laissez-faire is finished'.[2] Peer Steinbrück, then German finance minister, saw even broader changes in prospect: 'the US will lose its status as the super power of the world financial system. This world will become multi-polar . . . the world will never be as it was before the crisis.'[3] George Soros has used similar language. He criticizes politicians and central bankers on both sides of the Atlantic as being 'in the thrall of a market fundamentalist fallacy'.[4] In an earlier book, 'The Crisis of Global Capitalism'[5] Soros pinpointed the dominance of this fallacy as beginning in the early 1980s: 'it was only when Thatcher and Reagan came to power around 1980 that market fundamentalism became the dominant ideology'. Soros has consistently argued for re-regulation and for a reversal of the growing 'financialization' of western economies. Paul Krugman has advanced similar arguments, declaring in the summer of 2009 that 'deregulation bred bloated finance, which bred more deregulation, which bred this monster that ate the world economy'.[6]

The critique of laissez-faire finds a cousin in an attack on unfettered globalization. Katsuhito Iwai puts the case suc-cinctly in a paper called 'The Second End of Laissez-faire'. 'Globalization,' he argues, 'can be understood as a grand experiment to test the laissez-faire doctrine of neo-classical economics, which claims that a capitalist economy will become more efficient and stable as markets spread deeper and wider around the world. The "once a century" global economic crisis of 2007–9 stands as a testament to the failure of this grand experiment.'[7] Globalization did bring about a high level of average growth for the world as a whole, but at the same time it produced massive instability 'because capitalism is a system that is built essentially on speculation'. Others have gone back to the Brandt Commission report in 1980 which anticipated that unless governments corrected global monetary balances through coordinated global action, there would be a series of sovereign debt crises. The Commission's calls for reform of the world's monetary system look prescient today. As the crisis has evolved into a sovereign debt problem in many countries (notably Ireland, Greece and the UK) these arguments may look increasingly persuasive.[8]

Another strand of this critique has a more explicitly envi-ronmentalist flavour. Jacques Attali argues that 'the acute cause of the crisis is the growing difficulty the West has in compensating for its domestic depletion by attracting enough resources from elsewhere . . . the West instituted the globalization of markets in order to attract resources from the rest of the world, which made it possible for it to maintain its standard of living by creating a worldwide financial bubble.'[9] Jonathan Porritt, a British environmentalist, sees no difference between Tony Blair and Gordon Brown and Margaret Thatcher in this respect: 'they remain convinced to this day that economic success for any single nation depends entirely on the speed with which the global economy as a whole can be opened up to the full rigour of deregulated neo-liberalism.'[10] In his view, the original sin here is the pursuit of higher economic growth at all costs. Those arguments go beyond the scope of this book.

The response of those who might be expected to defend the set of beliefs which has informed their policies for some decades has been somewhat muted during the crisis. Gordon Brown, who in the past was loud in his praise of the City of London as a wealth creating engine for the UK economy as a whole, has switched to a language which emphasizes the role of technology and science-based innovation in promoting growth. Peter Mandelson, who in 1998, speaking of New Labour's attitudes, said 'we are intensely relaxed about people getting filthy rich, as long as they pay their taxes',[11] had changed tack by the time of the election campaign in 2010. Then he described Bob Diamond, the president of Barclays, as 'the unacceptable face of banking'.[12]

Others have stood their ground. In December 2009, Martin Feldstein rearticulated the defence of Reagan and Thatcher. In his view, even in the finance area 'financial deregulation made London a global financial centre. Some of those regulatory changes may be reversed but Britain is unlikely to jeopardize an important component of its economy by returning to pre-Thatcher financial rules . . . policies do evolve as conditions change and as we learn from experience. But the dramatic policy changes in the US and Britain under Ronald Reagan and Margaret Thatcher brought about such profound improvements that there is no going back.'[13] Niall Ferguson has similarly cautioned against overreaction, and drawing the wrong lessons. In a robust response to Paul Krugman's critique he argued that 'we're going to get the 1970s for fear of the 1930s'.[14]

In the summer of 2010 these arguments continued to ebb

and flow, though the leaders of the advanced industrialized countries had toned down their rhetoric in favour of more practical reform measures on the one hand, and denunciation of the greed and fecklessness of bankers on the other. But some of the underlying tensions in the global economy remained – imbalances being one very visible element. The policy responses of 2007–2010, which helped to prevent the recession turning into a depression, left many governments with huge fiscal deficits. The consequences of necessary efforts to reduce those deficits in the coming years will be severe for the public sectors of those countries, and are likely to constrain real wage growth elsewhere, too. So popular criticism of financialization and globalization may continue to be a prominent feature of politics for some time, with unpredictable consequences for economic policy.

References

1. How we all lost when Thatcher won. Billy Bragg. 5 March 2009. www.guardian.co.uk
2. 'Laissez-faire' capitalism is finished, says France. Elitsa Vucheva. EUObserver. 26 September 2008. http://euobserver.com
3. Ibid.
4. The false belief at the heart of the financial turmoil. George Soros. 3 April 2008. *The Financial Times*. www.ft.com
5. *The Crisis of Global Capitalism*. George Soros. Public Affairs. 1998.
6. The Crisis and How to Deal with It. *The New York Review of Books*. 11 June 2009. www.nybooks.com
7. The Second End of Laissez-Faire: The Bootstrapping Nature of Money and the Inherent Instability of Capitalism. Katsuhito Iwai. October 2009. CIRJE Discussion Paper No. 646. www.e.u-tokyo.ac.jp
8. How the Brandt Report Foresaw Today's Global Economic Crisis. James Quilligan. *Integral Review*, Vol. 6, No. 1. March 2010.
9. Jacques Attali in *The Future of Money*, ed. Oliver Chittenden. Virgin Books. 2010.
10. Jonathon Porritt, in the above.
11. Peter Mandelson. *The Financial Times*. 23 October 1998. www.ft.com
12. Lord Mandelson attacks Barclays head. 3 April 2010. www.news. bbc.co.uk
13. Is the Reagan-Thatcher Revolution Over? Martin Feldstein. Project Syndicate. 9 December 2009. www.project-syndicate.org
14. *Crisis of Global Capitalism*, Soros.

2

THE RICH GET RICHER –
THE POOR BORROW

The growth of leverage in American households, in particular, is universally accepted as one of the underlying causes
of the crisis. But why did this leverage grow? Why were US
households so willing to take on additional debt, when the
long-term risks to their economic welfare should have been
apparent?

One explanation has come from economists on the left of
the political spectrum. A report for the president of the UN
General Assembly, prepared by a group chaired by Joseph
Stiglitz, put the point starkly. Their answer is that growing
income inequality is the underlying cause. Globalization has
been associated with increasing inequality of income, not
only within developing countries, but also among developing
countries and between developed and developing countries.[1]
In the advanced countries, 'median wages stagnated during
the last quarter century, while income inequalities surged
in favour of the upper quintiles of the income distribution
. . . The negative impact of stagnant real incomes and rising
income inequality on aggregate demand was largely offset by
financial innovation and lax monetary policy that increased the
ability of households to finance consumption by borrowing.'
In countries where income inequality increased less, which
was the case in parts of continental Europe, 'social protection
systems . . . provided partial compensation for stagnating

income' and 'were financed through increased public deficits and public debt'.

The report argued, for good measure, that the Iraq war played a part in pushing up the price of oil which brought further reduction in purchase power in many countries.

Others have developed this line further. Branko Milanovic of the Carnegie Endowment for International Peace notes that middle-class income stagnation became a recurrent theme in American political life, and 'an insoluble political problem for both Democrats and Republicans . . . A way to make it seem that the middle class was earning more than it did was to increase its purchasing power through broader and more accessible credit . . . High net-worth individuals and the financial sector were . . . keen to find new lending opportunities . . . The middle class and those poorer than them were happy to see their tight budget constraint removed . . . and partake in the longest US post World War II economic expansion.'[2]

Thomas Palley of the New America Foundation broadens the critique to one of the entire neo-liberal growth model which has underpinned American economic policy for decades.[3] Debt and asset price inflation drove demand, in place of wage growth. 'A second flaw was the model of US engagement with the global economy that created a triple economic haemorrhage of spending on imports, manufacturing job losses, and off-shoring of investment.' Deregulation and financial excess are not the ultimate cause of the crisis. Instead, the US needs a new economic paradigm and a new growth model which involves rethinking its commitment to unfettered globalization.

These arguments are strongly contested by others. While Chairman Bernanke of the Fed has himself recognized the growth in income inequality as an important economic phenomenon, his view is that 'the influence of globalization on inequality has been moderate and almost surely less important than the effects of skill-based technological change'.[4] Others also challenge the data on rising income inequality. Kruger and Perry note that 'consumption inequality . . . has remained substantially stable'.[5] Steven Levitt in 'Freakonomics'[6] argues that 'the prices of goods that poor people tend to consume have fallen sharply relative to the prices of goods that rich people consume. Consequently, when you measure the true buying power of the rich and the poor, inequality grew only one-third as fast as economists previously thought it did — or maybe didn't grow at all.' Furthermore, there is evidence that higher-income households are particularly vulnerable to fluctuation in aggregate consumption. Their vulnerability has increased in recent years and high-income households currently 'bear an inordinately large share of aggregate fluctuations'.[7] So the crisis may well have a significant impact on smoothing consumption inequality.

But these analyses do not challenge the broad picture of rising income inequality, as measured by the Gini index. And the data shows that incomes of the top 5 per cent and top 1 per cent of households have risen much more sharply than those in the bottom half of the distribution, for many years. The top 5 per cent of US households earned 15 per cent of total household income in 1980; by 2006 that share had risen to 21.5 per cent. In the UK household borrowing similarly rose rapidly, and income inequality has also increased dramatically over the last three decades. Very big increases in the pay of the top 1 per cent of the income distribution have been driven largely by bankers' bonuses.[8]

In addition to the possible effect on households' propensity to borrow, Lorenzo Bini Smaghi of the European Central Bank points to an impact on political attitudes to the financial sector, and particularly to government policy towards failing institutions. He sees growing income inequality as one of the reasons why the US authorities were not prepared to rescue Lehman Brothers, noting that 'the emergence of stark inequalities entails the risk that decision-making mechanisms will be blocked, in particular in crisis situations, with negative repercussions for the collective good and social cohesion'.[9]

References

1. Report of the Commission of Experts of the President of the United Nations General Assembly on Reforms of the International Monetary and Financial System. New York. September 2009. www.un.org

2. The True Origins of the Financial Crisis. Branko Milanovic. Yale Global Online. 12 May 2009. http://yaleglobal.yale.edu
3. America's Exhausted Paradigm: Macroeconomic Causes of the Financial Crisis and Great Recession. Thomas Palley. New America Foundation. June 2009. www.newamerica.net
4. The Level and Distribution of Economic Well-Being. Ben Bernanke. Speech before the Greater Omaha Chamber of Commerce. 6 February 2007. www.federalreserve.gov
5. Inequality in what? Dirk Krueger and Fabrizio Perri. 16 February 2007. www.cato-unbound.org
6. Shattering the Conventional Wisdom on Growing Inequality. Steven Levitt. Freakonomics Blog. 19 May 2008. http://freakonomics.blogs.nytimes.com
7. Who Bears Aggregate Fluctuations and How? Jonathan Parker and Annette Vissing-Jorgensen. NBER Working Paper No. 14665. January 2009. www.nber.org
8. Centre of Economic Performance Analysis. May 2010. www.cep.lse.ac.uk
9. Some Thoughts on the International Financial Crisis. Lorenzo Bini Smaghi. Speech at the Unione Cristiana Imprenditori e Dirigenti. Milan. 20 October 2008. www.ecb.eu

3

THE SAVINGS GLUT
GLOBAL IMBALANCES

A striking feature of the world economy in the years before the crisis was the build-up of huge current account imbalances. In 2006 the combined current account deficit of the US and some other advanced economies was around $800 billion, while the surplus run by the oil-exporters, China and Japan was slightly larger. These imbalances had persisted for some years but expanded rapidly from 2002 onwards. There continues to be a chicken and egg style controversy about who is most responsible for the generation of these imbalances. Was it chronic over-consumption on the part of the United States, or chronic over-production, facilitated by a manipulated exchange rate, on the part of China? This controversy continues to divide opinion among economists, but it is rather the consequences of the imbalances that concern us here.

Richard Portes maintains that 'global macroeconomic imbalances are the underlying cause of the crisis'.[1] Ben Bernanke of the Federal Reserve has said 'in my view . . . it is impossible to understand the crisis without reference to the global imbalances in trade and capital flows that began in the latter half of the 1990s'.[2] In his statement before the G20 summit in Washington in November 2008, Hank Paulson, then US Treasury Secretary, referred to 'global imbalances that fuelled recent excesses'. While the G20 leaders did not agree on the origins of the imbalances, they nonetheless noted that 'inconsistent and insufficiently coordinated macroeconomic policies' had led to 'unsustainable global macroeconomic outcomes. These developments, together, contributed to excesses and ultimately resulted in severe market disruptions.'[3] The unusual term 'unsustainable global macroeconomic outcomes' reflected Chinese opposition to an explicit reference to imbalances.[4]

What is the mechanism through which these imbalances are thought to have led to the crisis?

Essentially, the United States was able to increase its debt dramatically without suffering from an inability to finance it. Surplus countries continued to buy US government securities, driving down long-term rates. The Chinese have now accumulated some $2.5 trillion of US treasuries. The imbalances gave rise to what has been called a 'savings glut' in developing countries which held interest rates low. That, in turn, caused investors to look for higher returns on other assets. Investors sought bond-like instruments offering a spread above the risk-free rate, in an attempt to offset the declines in that rate. That demand for yield was met by a wave of financial innovation, centred on the creation of securitized debt instruments, offering apparent security but nonetheless at a somewhat higher yield. This process drove up the capital values of risky instruments across the board. The risk premium on high yield bonds fell, in the years immediately before the crisis, to around half its long-term average.

The impact of this excess liquidity was not offset by monetary policy (Section 4). Central Banks focusing on retail price inflation took comfort from the fact that it remained low, held down by competitive imports from China and elsewhere (their competitiveness assisted, some would say, by an artificially low exchange rate).

How could these imbalances have persisted for so long? One thesis is that weaknesses in the Bretton Woods system allowed it. A country that issues assets which have reserve status around the world (as is the case with the United States) can finance current account deficits for an extended period. A second flaw is that a country facing upward pressure on the value of its currency can manage its exchange rate to resist such pressure and delay adjustment in its balance of payments. These two features of the system mean that apparently unsustainable imbalances can continue for far longer than might seem possible. But, on the principle that if a thing cannot go on forever it will probably end one day, there was bound to be a reckoning. That reckoning took a more dramatic form than even those who had warned about these imbalances, which included several Central Banks, the BIS, and the IMF, had suspected.

Considerable support for this line of argument has emerged in the last three years. Obstfeld and Rogoff, in a thorough exploration of the relationship between imbalances and the crisis, argue that the two are intimately connected.[5] They note that the US ability to finance macroeconomic imbalances through easy foreign borrowing allowed it to postpone tough policy choices. Foreign banks provided a ready source of external funding for the US deficit. So they see the imbalances as a symptom of flawed macroeconomic policy, rather than the cause of the crisis. But they conclude 'in effect, the global imbalances posed stress tests for weaknesses in the United States, British, and other advanced country financial and political systems – tests that those countries did not pass'. As a result, Greenspan's forecast that while the deficit could not widen for ever, the 'flexibility of the American economy will likely facilitate any adjustment without significant consequences to aggregate economic activity'[6] turned out to be well wide of the mark.

Not everyone agrees. Ricardo Caballero of MIT and Arvind Krishnamurthy, for example, argue that 'the root imbalance was not the global imbalance but a safe assets imbalance: The entire world . . . had an insatiable demand for safe debt instruments which put an enormous pressure on the US financial system.'[7] It was this demand for safe assets that stimulated the securitization boom, and the creation of synthetic AAA instruments.

Whatever the precise order of causation between flawed macroeconomic policies, large current account imbalances and investor demand for apparently low risk assets nonetheless yielding an attractive return, it seems clear that this combination played a significant part in the build-up to the crisis. It allowed the creation of leverage on a massive scale. But it was the interaction between the excess liquidity and financial innovation on the one hand, and monetary policy on the other, which produced a highly combustible mixture.

References

1. Global Imbalances. Richard Portes. In *Macroeconomic Stability and Financial Regulation: Key Issues for the G20*, ed. Mathias Dewatripoint, Xavier Freixas and Richard Portes. Centre for Economic and Policy Research. London. 2009.
2. A Conversation with Ben Bernanke. Conference at the Council on Foreign Relations. 10 March 2009. www.cfr.org
3. Statement from the G-20 Summit on Financial Markets and the World Economy. 15 November 2008. www.g20.org
4. Global Imbalances and the Financial Crisis. Steven Dunaway. Council of Foreign Relations Special Report No. 44. March 2009. www.cfr.org
5. Global Imbalances and the Financial Crisis: Products of Common Causes. Maurice Obstfeld and Kenneth Rogoff. CEPR Discussion Paper No. 7606. December 2009. www.cepr.org
6. Remarks by Chairman Alan Greenspan at Advancing Enterprise Conference. 4 February 2005. www.federalreserve.gov
7. Global Imbalances and Financial Fragility. Ricardo Caballero and Arvind Krishnamurthy. *American Economic Review*. May 2009.

4

TOO LOOSE FOR TOO LONG – US MONETARY POLICY

The second leg of the argument that macroeconomic conditions were crucial contributors to the crisis centres on the role of monetary policy, especially in the United States. Those who attach some blame to the Federal Reserve do not necessarily think that other factors – greedy bankers, reckless innovation, sleepy regulators – were unimportant. They believe, however, that monetary policy effectively creates the climatic conditions within which financial markets operate. When the weather is foggy, or there is much ice and snow on the road, driving behaviour which might otherwise reflect a reasonable balance between speed and prudence leads to more accidents and sometimes to an unpleasant pile-up.

There are many who believe that the Fed's interest rate policy in the early years of the century was too loose. They may give Alan Greenspan credit for relaxing policy aggressively after the dot-com bust and the Twin Towers attack, but they believe he was subsequently too slow to tighten. Between 2000 and 2003 the Fed lowered the Federal Funds target rate from 6.5 per cent to 1 per cent and did not begin to tighten until July 2004, and even then very cautiously. This long period of low short-term rates created very loose credit conditions, especially when seen in conjunction with the large inflow of savings from overseas. It was not therefore a surprise that house prices rose consistently throughout that period. By 2006 the Fed's tightening may have contributed to the deflation of the housing bubble, but this was too late to prevent a rout in the securitization market.

John Taylor, a professor of economics at Stanford and formerly in the US Treasury, is a strong proponent of this argument. Taylor is the eponymous creator of the so-called Taylor rule, which uses three variables: the inflation rate, GDP growth and the interest rate, to predict monetary policy. Although the Federal Reserve does not explicitly follow the Taylor rule, over time it has been a reasonably accurate descriptor of how US monetary policy has been conducted. Taylor calculates that the Federal Funds rate dropped significantly below the rate predicted by his rule from the end of 2001 and remained significantly below until 2006. He notes that this deviation of policy from the rule is unusually large, larger than at any time since the 1970s. He sees this as 'clear evidence of monetary excesses during the period leading up to the housing boom'.[1]

He calculates that the interest rate deviation was likely to bring about a reduction in housing starts and house price inflation and believes that this monetary policy argument is more persuasive than the 'global savings glut' thesis. While he acknowledges that there was a sizeable influx of savings from overseas, the US was saving less than it was investing, so the 'positive saving gap outside the United States was offset by an equal sized saving gap in the US'. Deliberately low interest rates, combined with other government interventions in the housing market through Fannie Mae and Freddie Mac, directly led to the housing boom and subsequent subprime bust.

Alan Greenspan has explicitly rejected this argument.[2] In his view, 'it was long-term interest rates that galvanized home asset prices, not the overnight rates of Central Banks'. The housing bubble was driven by the low level of the thirty-years fixed-rate mortgage, which 'had clearly delinked from the fed funds rate in the early part of this decade'. He contests Taylor's argument that housing starts may be used as a measure of the boom as 'evidence suggests that it is not starts that drive prices and initiate the "upward spiral", but the other way around'. He accepts that central banks could have attempted to deflate the bubble, but only at a price. 'There are no examples, to my knowledge, of a successful incremental defusing of a bubble that left prosperity intact.' He does acknowledge that earlier interest rises would have had an impact, but 'we never had a sufficiently strong conviction about the risks that could lie ahead . . . we had been lulled into a state of complacency. Given history, we believed that any declines in home prices would be gradual. Destabilizing debt problems were not perceived to arise under those conditions.' Even after the major disruptions of the last three years, Greenspan maintains that a central bank cannot hope to puncture episodes of rational exuberance: 'Unless there is a societal choice to abandon dynamic markets and leverage for some form of central planning, I fear that preventing bubbles will in the end turn out to be infeasible. Assuaging their aftermath seems the best we can hope for.'[3]

This pessimistic and minimalist view of the possible impact of the central bank is explicitly rejected by many others. In several papers, some dating from well before the onset of the crisis, William White and Claudio Borio, formerly and currently of the Bank for International Settlements respectively, have strongly argued that central banks should take account of credit conditions and asset price bubbles in calibrating their monetary policy. They think that a narrow focus on retail price inflation is likely to give a misleading reading of financial conditions. Since central banks typically have either an explicit or implicit responsibility for maintaining financial stability, they should take account of financial conditions more broadly. That may well mean 'leaning against the wind' of asset price bubbles. White and Borio drew attention to the risk of financial instability in the years before the crisis, but their arguments for pre-emptive action were rejected by central bankers at the time, and notably by Alan Greenspan.[4] (For an extended discussion on the case for and against leaning against the wind, and a broader approach to monetary policy, see Davies and Green.[5])

The arguments of the 'leaners' have become stronger as the economic damage caused by the crisis has grown. Greenspan's point that bubbles cannot be popped without some cost to output is accepted. But the cost of pre-emptive action may be lower than the cost of allowing the bubble to inflate and simply 'mopping up' afterwards. His view that it is impossible to identify bubbles as they inflate is also disputed. There can be no certainty about bubbles, but nor can one be certain about other judgements which go into the monetary policy decision, such as the rate of growth of capacity in the economy and any potential output gap. Goodhart and others[6] have canvassed a range of indicators which might be used to give early warnings of market exuberance and price misalignments.

This remains highly controversial territory. Bringing credit and asset prices into the definition of the objectives of monetary policy would require a significant recalibration of inflation target regimes such as those operated in the United Kingdom. Defenders of the simplicity of inflation targeting note the risk of a loss of explanatory power and influence on expectations if the Central Bank seeks to influence a broader range of variables than retail prices. Others think the crisis has made narrow inflation targeting unsustainable in the future. The European Central Bank maintains that its monetary pillar is a useful way of taking financial conditions into account. Others think that if there is any leaning against the wind to be done, it should be a task for macroprudential supervision, which allows for more close targeting of credit provision to different asset classes. This debate has further to run.

References

1. *Getting Off Track*. John Taylor. Hoover Institution Press. 2009.
2. The Crisis. Alan Greenspan. Brookings Paper on Economic Activity. Spring 2010. www.brookings.edu
3. Ibid.
4. Should Monetary Policy 'Lean or Clean'? William White. Federal Reserve Bank of Dallas Working Paper No. 34. August 2009. www.dallasfed.org; also The Brave New World of Central Banking. Stephen Cecchetti. Working Paper Series of the Czech National Bank No. 14. December 2005. www.cnb.cz
5. *Banking on the Future: The Fall and Rise of Central Banking*. Howard Davies and David Green. Princeton University Press. 2010.
6. How to avoid the next crash. Charles Goodhart and Avinash Persaud. *The Financial Times*. 30 January 2008. www.ft.com

B   THE TRIGGER

The first four analyses discuss the underlying causes of the unstable markets which erupted in 2007. They do not explain what triggered the explosion. The next two explanations offer answers to the 'Why then?' question.

The first (Section 5) explores a general 'financial instability hypothesis' which may explain the build-up of tensions in the system.

The second (6) examines the catalyst for the 2007 crisis – the rapid collapse of the subprime mortgage securitization market – and considers the role of government in promoting the development of that market. Was this a financial market phenomenon, driven by greedy brokers and bankers, or the reflection of unwise political intervention?

5

MINSKY'S MOMENT

In August 2007, *The Wall Street Journal* proclaimed on its front page that while investors and banks around the world were suffering, the stock of a little-known economist who died a decade earlier was on the rise. Hyman Minsky 'spent much of his career advancing the idea that financial systems are inherently susceptible to bouts of speculation that, if they last long enough, end in crises'.[1] In 'The Financial Instability Hypothesis',[2] published in 1992, he describes the mechanisms which lead to a financial crisis.

Minsky classifies the financing of illiquid investments into three categories: hedge finance, speculative finance and Ponzi finance. Hedge financing is the typical form used in the early stages of a business cycle. Hedge financing units are those which can fulfil all of their contractual payment obligations by their cash flows. In speculative financing the borrower knows that the cash outflows will exceed the inflows at some future date, even though over the life of the asset enough cash will be generated to pay for the investment. These arrangements need to roll over their liabilities at some point. If at the time of the expected rollover no re-financing is available, the borrower may turn to Ponzi financing. In Minsky's words, 'for Ponzi units, the cash flows from operations are not sufficient to fulfil either the repayment of principal or the interest due on outstanding debts. Such units can sell assets or borrow.

Borrowing to pay interest or selling assets to pay interest (and even dividends) on common stock lowers the equity of a unit, even as it increases liabilities and the prior commitment of future incomes.' He argues that when speculative finance turns into Ponzi finance, investors with cash flow shortfalls will be forced to sell. 'This is likely to lead to a collapse of asset values.'

In 1998, Paul McCulley of Pimco coined the phrase 'Minsky moment' which was the point in the cycle when investors experience cash flow problems and begin to sell down, leading to a sudden collapse in market prices and a sharp drop in liquidity. He used the phrase initially to describe the 1998 Russian financial crisis, but Minsky's characterization also appeared to capture well what had happened in the subprime market.

Not everyone is persuaded that the Minsky hypothesis describes the subprime crisis. Paul Davidson[3] argues that 'Minsky's speculative finance operation is never available to subprime borrowers. To create a Minsky moment in the subprime situation, therefore, the only alternative would be for the subprime debtor-purchaser to engage in Ponzi finance.' But most subprime borrowers have little or no equity in their homes, so the Ponzi finance operation was never a viable option for them.

Frank Shostak of the Ludwig Von Mises Institute also rejects the notion that Minsky's framework is relevant. He notes that 'the heart of Minsky's framework is that capitalism is inherently unstable and has self-destructive tendencies. An important mechanism for this destructive tendency is the accumulation of debt. Contrary to Minsky, our analysis shows that it is the existence of the central bank that makes modern capitalism unstable. It is this factor alone that is responsible for the current financial instability.'[4] It is the government's interventions in the market, through the central bank, that allow the financial system to engage in the reckless expansion of credit.

Nonetheless, much of the financial system remediation work underway since 2007 has been predicated on the assumption that modern financial markets are prone to speculative bubbles, and that the central banking and regulatory disciplines on the market have not been effective in leaning against those speculative cycles, whether they are Minsky-like, or of a different character.

References

1. In Time of Tumult, Obscure Economist Gains Currency. Justin Lahart. *The Wall Street Journal*. 18 August 2007. http://wsj.com
2. The Financial Instability Hypothesis. Hyman Minsky. Levy Economics Institute Economics Working Paper No. 74. www.levy.org
3. Is the current financial distress caused by the subprime mortgage crisis a Minsky moment? Paul Davidson. *Journal of Post-Keynesian Economics*, Vol. 30, No. 4. 2008.
4. Does the Current Financial Crisis Vindicate the Economics of Hyman Minsky? Frank Shostak. Mises Daily. 27 November 2007. http://mises.org

6

THE SUBPRIME COLLAPSE: A FAILURE OF GOVERNMENT?

While politicians and commentators on the left have argued that the crisis reflects a failure of laissez-faire capitalism and unregulated markets, those on the right have looked for an alternative explanation, seeing the nefarious influence of government manipulation of markets as the true underlying cause. They begin from the assumption that free markets have inbuilt corrective mechanisms. If those mechanisms did not operate properly, then it is probable that they were overridden by political or social interventions. In the specific case of the subprime crisis, it is argued that a range of government mechanisms and influences pressed financial firms to make imprudent loans.

The argument has been summarized by Professor Thomas Di Lorenzo of Loyola College: 'the thousands of mortgage defaults and foreclosures in the subprime housing market are the direct result of 30 years of government policy that has forced banks to make bad loans to un-creditworthy borrowers.' The policy in question is the 1977 Community Reinvestment Act (CRA), which compels banks to make loans to low-income borrowers, and what the supporters of the Act call 'communities of colour', that they might not otherwise make based on purely economic criteria.[1]

A variant of this argument, which is sometimes presented as complementary to it, is that the government-supported entities (GSEs), Fannie Mae and Freddie Mac, facilitated the rapid expansion of the subprime market in the early years of the century by being prepared to buy up the resulting mortgages on a massive scale. Those purchases led to the very costly collapse of the two GSEs, which were effectively nationalized (technically put into a conservatorship) in September 2008.

It is certainly the case that, over an extended period, a variety of US government policies, under administrations of both parties, were focused on attempting to correct what were perceived to be inequities in the mortgage market, which resulted in significantly lower percentages of home ownership among ethnic minority communities. In 1985, while the home ownership rate in the US as a whole was 64.3 per cent, among the black community it was only 44.4 per cent.[2] (In spite of a number of interventions, by 2005, while the home ownership rate in both communities had risen, the gap between the black and white percentages was even wider.) A Federal Reserve study concluded that mortgage-lending discrimination was systemic and that 'discrimination may be observed when a lender's underwriting policies contain arbitrary or outdated criteria that effectively disqualify many urban or lower-income minority applicants'.[3] It is argued that the use of the CRA to attempt to correct this imbalance led to the crisis. 'If the CRA had not been so aggressively pushed,' said Robert Litan of the Brookings Institution, 'it is conceivable things might not be as bad. People have to be honest about that.'[4]

The main provision of the CRA is that 'regulated financial institutions have continuing and affirmative obligation to help meet the credit needs of the local communities in which they are chartered'.[5] Banking regulators are required to consider an institution's record of meeting the credit needs of its community, including low- and moderate-income neighbourhoods, 'consistent with the safe and sound operation of such institution'.[6] Typically they will produce guidelines for the percentage of an institution's assets that should be represented by loans to the local community. This legislation had been in existence for over two decades before the subprime lending boom began, but it is argued that its influence, promoted by regulation, became more pronounced in the late 1990s.

In the face of these criticisms, the Federal Reserve has examined the record. Their conclusions were reported in a speech by then Governor Randy Kroszner in December 2008.[7] His view was that the CRA had not contributed to the erosion of safe and sound lending practices. He reported Federal Reserve studies which, perhaps surprisingly, found that 'lending to lower-income individuals and communities has been nearly as profitable and performed similarly to other types of lending done by CRA covered institutions'. They found that 'the loans that are the focus of the CRA represent a very small proportion of the subprime lending market . . . and that CRA related subprime loans performed in a comparable manner to other subprime loans'. Furthermore, 'most foreclosure filings have taken place in middle- or higher-income neighbourhoods: in fact, foreclosure filings have increased at a faster pace in middle- or higher-income areas than in lower-income areas that are the focus of the CRA'. Only 6 per cent of all the higher priced (subprime) loans were extended by CRA covered lenders to lower-income borrowers or neighbourhoods. This, according to Kroszner, 'makes it hard to imagine how this law could have contributed, in any meaningful way, to the current subprime crisis'.

The case in relation to Fannie Mae and Freddie Mac is more complex. In 1995 they began to receive tax incentives for purchasing mortgage-backed securities which included loans to low-income borrowers. In 1996, the Department of Housing & Urban Development set a goal that at least 42 per cent of the mortgages they purchased should be to borrowers with below-median household incomes. That new requirement was explicitly linked to lending to minorities. So William Apgar, an aide to Andrew Cuomo, then the HUD Secretary, said 'we believe that there are a lot of loans to black Americans that could be safely purchased by Fannie Mae and Freddie Mac if these companies were more flexible'.[8] Franklin Raines, then the Chairman of Fannie Mae, said 'we have not been a major presence in the subprime market, but you can bet that under these goals, we will be'.[9] *The New York Times* presciently suggested at the time that, 'in moving, even tentatively, into this new area of lending, Fannie Mae is taking on significantly more risk, which may not pose any difficulties during flush economic times. But, the government subsidized corporation may run into trouble in an economic downturn, prompting a government rescue similar to that of the savings and loan industry in the 1980s.'[10]

From that time, the involvement of the two GSEs in subprime lending grew. From small beginnings in the late 1990s, in 2006 Fannie Mae and Freddie Mac purchased around $175 billion of subprime securities. By 2008, the two GSEs owned $5.1 trillion in residential mortgages, about half the US mortgage market, with a large proportion of them subprime loans which collapsed in value.

Did the involvement of the two GSEs have a decisive influence on the growth of the subprime market? Paul Krugman thinks not: 'Fannie and Freddie had nothing to do with the explosion of high-risk lending . . . in fact, Fannie and Freddie, after growing rapidly in the 1990s, largely faded from the scene during the height of the housing bubble . . . whatever bad incentives the implicit federal guarantee creates have been offset by the fact that Fannie and Freddie were and are tightly regulated with regard to the risks they can take.'[11]

Others argue that the facts point to a different conclusion. By the summer of 2008, Fannie Mae had guaranteed subprime and Alt-A loans with an unpaid principal balance of $553 billion. They were over 20 per cent of its total mortgage book, around the percentage of subprime mortgages in the market as a whole. The same was broadly true of Freddie Mac.[12] And in September 2008, the Director of their new regulator, the Federal Housing Finance Agency, told Congress that these loans were the main reason for the GSEs' collapse: 'Fannie Mae and Freddie Mac purchased and guaranteed many more low documentation, low verification, and non-standard mortgages in 2006 and 2007 than they had in the past. Roughly 33% of the company's business involved buying or guaranteeing these risky mortgages, compared with 14% in 2005.'[13]

It is notable, too, that the Federal Reserve had earlier expressed public concerns about the growth of the GSEs and their influence on the total market. So in 2004, Chairman Greenspan proposed 'limiting the dollar amount of their debt relative to the dollar amount of mortgages securitized and held by their investors . . . to remove most of the potential systemic risk associated with the GSEs'.[14] These warnings were ignored, suggesting that there was political momentum behind the agencies' activities, which insulated them from criticism.

References

1. Did Liberals Cause the Subprime Crisis? Robert Gordon. *The American Prospect*. 7 April 2008. www.prospect.org/
2. State of the Nation's Housing 2008. Joint Center for Housing Studies. Harvard University. 2008. www.jchs.harvard.edu
3. Closing the Gap: A Guide to Equal Opportunity Lending. Federal Reserve Bank of Boston. 1993.
4. Did Liberals Cause the Subprime Crisis?, Gordon.
5. Housing and Community Development Act of 1977 – Title VIII on Community Reinvestment. www.fdic.gov
6. Ibid.
7. The Community Reinvestment Act and the Recent Mortgage Crisis. Governor Randall S. Kroszner. Speech on 3 December 2008 at the Board of Governors of the Federal Reserve System, Washington, DC. www.federalreserve.gov
8. Andrew Cuomo and Fannie and Freddie. Wayne Barrett. *Village Voice*. 5 August 2008. www.villagevoice.com/
9. Community Reinvestment Act, Kroszner.
10. Fannie Mae Eases Credit to Aid Mortgage Lending. Steven A. Holmes. *The New York Times*. 30 September 1999. www.nytimes.com/
11. The Last Trillion-Dollar Commitment: The Destruction of Fannie Mae and Freddie Mac. Peter J. Wallison and Charles W. Calomiris. American Enterprise for Public Policy Research. September 2008. www.aei.org
12. Ibid.
13. Ibid.
14. Fannie Mae Eases Credit, Holmes.

C THE FAILURES OF REGULATION

Whatever the underlying political and economic dynamics, should not regulators have done more to head off the problems, or at least to make the system more resistant to stress? Why did so many banks fail, or come close to doing so, when the market turned down?

There is a series of potential explanations which centre on global rules for bank capital and liquidity. There was too little capital in the system (Section 7), the rules were procyclical (8), and they missed the risks inherent in off-balance sheet vehicles (9). Liquidity, a central feature of the critics for the last three years, has been neglected by regulators intentionally (10).

The US regulatory system came in for particularly acute criticism, on several grounds: its complexity (11), the failure of the SEC to regulate investment banks effectively (12), the deregulation of derivatives markets around the turn of the century (13), the Federal Reserve's failure to regulate mortgage selling (14) and the repeal of the Glass-Steagall Act (15). The latter had encouraged the creation of institutions which were 'Too Big To Fail' (16).

In the UK, too, regulators were attacked. They, and the government, were accused of adopting an excessively light-touch approach (17). The institutional structure, introduced in 1997 with the separation of bank regulation from the Bank of England, and the creation of the FSA, was also criticized (18).

Globally, the system was seen by some to have failed to keep up with the growing integration of financial markets (19) and to have allowed 'black holes' in the form of weakly regulated offshore centres (20).

7

A CAPITAL SHORTAGE

The ultimate cost to the public purse of the bailouts is still uncertain, and share sales may prove profitable, but in the US and the UK, not to mention Ireland and Iceland, governments were obliged to commit a material fraction of annual GDP to supporting their banks. This reflects the fact that the banks themselves had inadequate reserves to cope with the losses they have incurred, or expect to incur, on their loan portfolios and trading activities. While prudential regulation cannot hope to remove the possibility of bank failure entirely, the scale of the losses, and the number of banks that had to be rescued, suggest that banks were undercapitalized before the crisis. As Axel Weber, the president of the Deutsche Bundesbank, said, 'the crisis revealed that the overall level of capital that banks were required to hold was insufficient compared with the magnitude of the losses. At the same time, it became apparent that the loss-absorbing capacity of the capital held was too low.'[1]

Capital requirements for banks are governed by global accords developed by the Basel Committee on Banking Supervision. Technically, the accords apply only to internationally active banks, but they are widely used as the basis for bank capitalization around the world. The first accord, in 1998, provided that banks should hold at least 8 per cent of capital, divided into two sub-categories, Tiers I and II. Tier I capital is principally shareholders' equity, while Tier II capital may be subordinated debt and a variety of other hybrid instruments. Under Basel I, a bank's portfolio was divided into a number of risk-weighted buckets, each with different capital requirements against them – less for sovereign debt, more for property lending, etc.

In the late 1990s, the Committee accepted that the Basel I 'by and large' approach was no longer adequate. Over the next decade it worked on a revised accord which was designed to be more risk-sensitive and to be based on three 'pillars'. The first pillar was a basic capital charge, the second pillar involved supervisory judgement to flex that charge depending on supervisors' assessment of the capability of the institution, while the third pillar (relatively underdeveloped) included a range of disclosure requirements. Surprisingly, in retrospect, the Committee spent little time on determining the overall quantum of capital, and Basel II was developed in the assumption that the total capital in the global banking system was 'about right', and that the accord would primarily focus on distributing that capital more appropriately. They also devoted little attention to the quality of capital. A range of hybrid instruments were accepted. The crisis showed that there, Tier II instruments were not effective buffers in stressed conditions. It was also agreed that sophisticated banks would be allowed to use their own risk models, validated by regulators, to determine their capital requirements. These models could be straightforward, or more advanced. Some were very complex indeed, but all were based on the risk modelling techniques.

Although some countries had implemented Basel II before the crisis struck, others, including the United States, had not done so. Some had supplemented Basel II with additional domestic requirements, such as leverage ratios which determined an overall maximum gearing for the balance sheet, whatever the outcome of the risk model assessment.

The crisis has revealed a number of weaknesses in this approach. A particular weakness, its procyclical construction, is discussed in Section 8. Section 26 explores the weaknesses of risk models which failed to capture the implications of long-tail events. But in addition to these flaws, it has been strongly argued that the level of capital which banks were required to hold was simply too low. As Philipp Hildebrand, now chairman of the Swiss National Bank, has explained, 'banks tend to hold very low levels of capital. In a cross-sectional comparison, banks have much lower capital cushions than uninsured firms. On average, listed non-financial firms have capital-to-asset ratios of 30 to 40 per cent. In stark contrast, before the onset of the current crisis, all of the world's top 50 banking institutions held, on average, only 4 per cent of capital.'[2] In part, this is simply a function of fractional reserve banking. But it also undoubtedly reflects the existence of safety nets in the forms of insured deposits and the potential for lender of last resort support supplied by the central banks.

In particular, the experience of the crisis has powerfully suggested that banks have been holding far too little capital to back their trading books. Capital requirements there have been low, on the grounds that hedging is effective, assets can rapidly be sold and positions unwound. That assumption proved to be invalid during the crisis.

As a result, the Basel Committee, prompted by the G20 and the Financial Stability Board, has proposed a significant enhancement of the capital regime, on which it is consulting during 2010. While the details remain to be resolved, the Committee has determined that 'the quality, consistency, and transparency of the capital base will be raised'.[3] The coverage of the capital framework will be strengthened to remove the incentives to move assets from the banking to the trading book and to take account of counterparty credit risk exposure arising from derivative, repos and securities financing activities. There will be a larger proportion of Tier I equity capital. Furthermore, the Committee has proposed to introduce a leverage ratio as a supplementary measure which 'will help contain the build-up of excessive leverage in the banking system, introduce additional safeguards against attempts to game the risk-based requirements, and help address model risk'. These measures, taken together, imply a very significant increase in capital reserves for many, if not all, banks. There are serious question marks about some of the detail, and about the ability of banks to raise this additional capital in the near term, so the requirements will certainly be phased and the quantum and timing remain to be determined.

Some changes are inevitable, and broadly agreed. But there remain three areas of controversy. First, will banks ever hold enough capital, given the existence of the safety net? Charles Calomiris of the Columbia Business School points to 'fundamental problems in measuring bank risk' and the difficulty of credibly enforcing effective discipline on large complex financial institutions. For the most significant institutions 'The too-big-to-fail problem magnifies incentives to take excessive risks; banks that expect to be protected by deposit insurance, Fed lending, and Treasury-Fed bailouts, and that believe that they are beyond discipline.'[4] He believes that additional capital will not be effective unless there are surcharges on large complex institutions and mechanisms to allow regulators to intervene and wind down large institutions, rather than simply bailing them out (Section 16). Resolution mechanisms are also on the agenda in many countries, but are by no means straightforward to introduce. There has been extensive debate on bank bankruptcy provisions for decades, but still no effective resolution of the intractable cross-border dimension.

A second concern relates to the impact of additional capital requirements. In principle, the risk of bank failure can be greatly reduced if bank capital requirements are raised to very high levels. But would this not be costly for the economy as a whole, as it would raise the cost of credit? Adair Turner of the UK FSA argues that the increased economic cost from high capital may be less than is often supposed, resting his case on the Modigliani–Miller view, which identifies that 'higher leverage cannot in the absence of tax effect reduce a firm's cost of capital, since as leverage increases both the cost of debt and the cost of equity will increase to reflect heightened risk'.[5] But capital requirements would reduce overall returns on banks' equity. Shareholders would need to appreciate that these low returns come with the benefit of lower risk.

Few would contest that stronger capitalization of banks is a lesson from the crisis. The financial markets themselves are likely to penalize weakly capitalized institutions, even if regulators do not do so. But the sums of new equity required to re-capitalize the system will be huge. The impact on credit availability and the cost of capital is uncertain. That impact is likely to be greater as the use of off-balance sheet vehicles and securitization is further constrained. Turner has persuasively argued that we need to consider future capital requirements in the context of a broader analysis of the role banks play in financing the real economy.[6]

References

1. Making the Financial System more Resilient – The Role of Capital Requirements. Axel Weber. Speech at Financial Services Ireland. Dublin. 10 March 2010. www.bundesbank.de
2. Is Basel II Enough? The Benefits of a Leverage Ratio. Philipp Hildebrand. Speech at the London School of Economics. London. 15 December 2008. www.lse.ac.uk
3. Strengthening the Resilience of the Banking Sector. Basel Committee on Banking Supervision. December 2009. www.bis.org
4. Bank Regulatory Reform in the Wake of the Financial Crisis. Charles Calomiris. April 2009. http://siteresources.worldbank.org
5. The Turner Review: A Regulatory Response to the Global Banking Crisis. Financial Services Authority. March 2009. www.fsa.gov.uk
6. What do Banks do, what should They do and what Public Policies are Needed to Ensure Best Results for the Real Economy? Speech by Adair Turner, Chairman. CASS Business School. 17 March 2010. www.fsa.gov.uk

8

PROCYCLICALITY

A related criticism is that capital requirements, in addition to being too low, were also procyclical; in other words they encouraged banks to hold too little capital in the upswing, and to hoard capital and cut back on lending sharply in the downturn, thus exaggerating the cycle and contributing to a credit crunch. It is argued that Basel II made this procyclicality more marked. The G20 Summit in London in April 2009 explicitly accepted this criticism, calling for changes to capital regulation 'to mitigate procyclicality, including the requirement for banks to build buffers of resources in good times that they can draw from when conditions deteriorate'.[1]

Regulators cannot hope to smooth the business cycle, and arguably should not attempt to do so. It is also inevitable that capital regulation will, to some extent, be procyclical. When determining the level of reserves a bank should hold, regulators look at the losses a bank would have incurred on its existing portfolio of assets in earlier years. So, for example, if house prices have been rising consistently, a portfolio of mortgages will seem to need less capital backing the higher prices rise. In a rising property market, even when borrowers default, lenders typically then recover the nominal value of the loan after repossession and sale.

In theory, at the peak of a very long boom cycle, a retrospective approach to modelling capital requirements will generate a very low number, just at the time when the risk of a sharp downward adjustment is highest.

Banking regulators are aware of this risk and in designing Basel II attempted to introduce 'through the cycle' methods of calculating the probability of loss and losses given default. Critics argued, however, that the methodology was flawed, on the grounds that 'changes in a bank's capital requirements over time would be only weakly correlated with changes in its economic capital, and there would be no means to infer economic capital from regulatory capital'.[2] The FSA in London has itself acknowledged that constructing cyclically adjusted figures is technically very challenging and that in general firms have not developed robust 'through the cycle' rating systems.[3]

While it is accepted that regulatory capital requirements do vary with the credit cycle, regulators argue that 'it is not clear . . . to what extent this *cyclicality* in the minimum capital requirement produces *procyclicality* in financial markets and broader economic activity.'[4] Furthermore, they point out that since Basel II came into effect in most large countries just before the crisis, and indeed has never been fully implemented in the United States, it is difficult to argue that Basel II itself was a decisive influence on the credit crisis.

The Financial Stability Board (FSB) accepts that 'the current financial crisis is a systemic event of large proportions that illustrates the destructive effects of procyclicality'.[5] But they argue that financial system procyclicality is traceable to two fundamental problems, which may be aggravated by pro-cyclical regulation, but which are not caused by it. The first problem they see is 'limitations in risk measurement', as measures of risk tend to be highly procyclical. They 'often spike once tensions arise, but may be quite low even as vul-nerabilities and risk build up during the expansion phase'. That is particularly true of credit risk in trading portfolios when measured over short holding periods 'using data that do not capture full credit cycles'. The second fundamental problem relates to incentives, and principal-agent issues. 'For example, collateral-based lending or margin requirements can protect lenders and traders from actions taken by borrowers and counterparties that could erode the value of their claims. But by establishing a direct link between asset valuations and funding, fluctuations in margin requirements can exacerbate procyclicality.' Furthermore, at times of stress, the actions of individual firms to withdraw credit and withhold liquidity can be self-defeating by inducing fire sales or a credit crunch.

Nonetheless, the FSB accepts that the introduction of higher risk sensitivity into capital requirements, as envisaged under Basel II, can mean that they move procyclically, 'they tend to fall during expansions, when measured risk is low, and rise possibly abruptly during contractions . . . this can amplify credit and business cycles and hence the risk of financial instability'. Their conclusion is that the Basel Committee 'should strengthen the regulatory capital framework so that the quality and level of capital in the banking system increase during strong economic conditions and can be drawn down during periods of economic and financial stress'.

This broad recommendation has attracted widespread support, but there has been less agreement on the mechanisms which can be used to deliver it. One now favoured approach is to introduce a so-called 'macroprudential mechanism', whereby supervisors would impose a surcharge on capital requirements, perhaps across all banks and all areas of business, or related to particular types of lending, such as mortgages, when overall financial conditions seem to suggest that there may be an asset price bubble. But the technology of determining when asset prices are in dangerously high territory is underdeveloped. Also, the interaction between macroprudential capital requirements and changes in interest rates has not been well articulated so far. So the degree to which capital requirements can be used as a tool to enhance the stability of the financial sector generally remains an open question.

The issues have been well debated by Borio in a paper published by the Banque de France.[6] He argues that the framework needs to rely as far as possible on automatic stabilizers, rather than discretion, to limit the risks of error by supervisors. But he also notes that 'any efforts to build up and release buffers in a credible way will need to address head-on a major issue: as strains materialize, markets may prevent the draw-down occurring'. He also notes that much policy attention has focused on procyclicality, and rather less on cross-sectional problems. The counter-cyclicality proposals 'are calibrated with respect to characteristics of the balance sheets of institutions on a standalone basis. They fail to take account of common liquidity exposures across institutions' (Section 10). So, on this analysis, procyclicality is not the only regulatory flaw, and perhaps not the most important one.

References

1. Declaration on Strengthening the Financial System – Annex to London Summit Communiqué. G20 Summit. 2 April 2009. www.g20. org
2. Procyclicality in Basel II: Can We Treat the Disease without Killing the Patient? Michael Gordy and Bradley Howells. *Journal of Financial Intermediation* No. 15. 2006.
3. A Regulatory Response to the Global Banking Crisis. Financial Services Authority. Discussion Paper 09/02. 2009. www.fsa.gov.uk
4. Reducing Procyclicality Arising from the Bank Capital Framework. Joint FSF-BCBS Working Group on Bank Capital Issues. www.financialstabilityboard.org
5. Addressing Procyclicality in the Financial System. Report of the Financial Stability Forum. April 2009. www.financialstabilityboard. org
6. Implementing the Macroprudential Approach to Financial Regulation and Supervision. Claudio Borio. *Financial Stability Review* No. 13. Banque de France. September 2009. www.banque-france.fr

9

THE CANARY IN THE COAL MINE

OFF-BALANCE SHEET VEHICLES

Securitized Investment Vehicles (SIVs) and conduits were early victims of the crisis. Several ran into funding difficulties in the summer of 2007. Some failed, others were rescued by the banks which had created them. By the end of 2008, the SIV market was essentially closed and almost all of the vehicles had been liquidated or taken over. SIVs were the 'canary in the coal mine' of the financial crisis. Or were they more than that, and did their growth and subsequent collapse contribute materially to the meltdown?

It is generally assumed that structured investment vehicles were invented by Citibank in 1988. The main role of these vehicles is to issue short maturity commercial paper to fund longer-term and lower quality assets, generating a profit on the spread between funding cost and investment return. SIVs were largely invested in longer maturity corporate bonds, while conduits, otherwise similar, were invested mainly in receivables, leases and loans. SIVs are typically tranched, like Collateralized Debt Obligations (CDOs). Many were created and sponsored by banks offering backup lines of credit in return for a share of the profits. Some of the vehicles in this category had well-diversified asset bases, but many had significant mortgage-related exposure, and specifically sub-prime exposure. When the commercial paper market seized up in the summer of 2007, they were unable to roll over their short-term funding. The market was aware that some had significant exposure to the subprime market, but the opacity of the structures meant there was considerable uncertainty about who was most exposed, which created a liquidity crisis in the market as a whole. Without a source of short-term funding, the vehicles faced liquidation. The investment banks, therefore, while perhaps technically not required to rescue them, typically did so partly for reputational reasons and partly to avoid a fire sale of assets which would have affected their own balance sheets.

The SIV market grew substantially in the years before the crisis. Standard & Poors' estimate that their total assets rose from $100 billion in 2003 to around $300 billion in early 2007. But they were part of a broader trend in growth in what is generally known as the 'shadow banking' market. Estimates suggest that the shadow banking market was, by 2007, around the same size as the asset base of the US commercial banking market, at some $7 trillion.[1] SIVs were, therefore, part of the phenomenon of very rapid credit growth which is at the centre of most plausible explanations of the crisis.

Some argue that they were a uniquely dangerous feature of the financial landscape and that they deserve a high ranking in the league table of culprits. Paul Krugman characterizes the run on the shadow banking system as being 'the core of what happened' to cause the crisis. 'As the shadow banking system expanded to rival or even surpass conventional banking in importance, politicians and government officials should have realized that they were recreating the kind of financial vulnerability that made the great depression possible – and they should have responded by extending regulations and the financial safety net to cover these new institutions. Influential figures should have proclaimed a simple rule: anything that does what a bank does, anything that has to be rescued in crises the way banks are, should be regulated like a bank.'[2]

In retrospect it is clear that many of these vehicles, particularly the SIVs, were created to get around existing accounting rules and regulatory capital standards. By holding assets off-balance sheet, investment and commercial banks avoided the sizable capital charges which would have been imposed on them had the assets been on balance sheet. As Adair Turner has pointed out, 'at the individual bank level, the classification of these as off-balance sheet proved inaccurate as a reflection of the true economic risk, with liquidity provision commitments and reputational concerns requiring many banks to take the assets back on balance sheet as the crisis grew, driving a significant one-off increase in measured leverage'.[3] In addition, the rapid growth of the shadow banking system more generally created conditions of much greater systemic financial vulnerability. On this analysis, we should welcome the disappearance of SIVs.

But others caution against a blanket condemnation. The Group of Thirty report on financial reform distinguished between vehicles which served no sustainable economic purpose other than leveraged arbitrage of capital rules, and those which are used to support the issuance of traditional asset-backed securitizations. They think a revival of the securitization markets will be necessary to provide for the credit needs of the global economy as it returns to growth. So while supporting accounting rule changes which push the consolidation of many types of off-balance sheet vehicles they say that 'it is important, before they are fully implemented, that careful consideration be given to how these rules are likely to impact efforts to restore the viability of securitized credit markets'.[4]

There is broad consensus that off-balance sheet vehicles were a material feature of the unstable financial conditions which precipitated the financial collapse. They highlighted the weaknesses of accounting rules which emphasized form over substance. They were exemplars of the kind of financial innovation whose long-term risks were poorly understood, and they demonstrated weaknesses in the way regulators and central banks assessed financial conditions, with too little emphasis placed on aggregate expansion of credit. As Paul Tucker of the Bank of England argues, 'the experience underlines a need for more transparency around key financing markets, transparency to which the central banks ought to be able to contribute as they stand at the centre of the markets in which these vehicles operated . . .' There is also, he argues, a need for 'macroprudential instruments that could be deployed to constrain excess by influencing banks' supply of credit to them'.[5]

References

1. A Vicious Circle of Credit Retention. BCA Research. February 2008. www.bcaresearch.com
2. *The Return of Depression Economics and the Crisis of 2008*. Paul Krugman. W. W. Norton Company Ltd. 2009.
3. The Turner Review: A Regulatory Response to the Global Banking Crisis. Financial Services Authority. March 2009. www.fsa.gov.uk
4. Final Reform: A Framework for Financial Stability. Group of Thirty's Working Group on Financial Reform. 2009. www.group30.org
5. Shadow Banking, Financing Markets and Financial Stability. Remarks by Paul Tucker at a BGC Partners Seminar, London. 21 January 2010. www.bankofengland.co.uk

10

THE TAXI AT THE STATION – LIQUIDITY

In the early summer of 2007, the cost of insuring subprime mortgages began to rise sharply. The ratings agencies put subprime-related securitizations on 'downgrade review', some hedge funds run by Bear Stearns had difficulty meeting margin calls and Countrywide Financial announced a sharp drop in earnings. By July, the market for short-term asset-backed commercial paper, an important source of liquidity for banks, began to dry up. IKB, a German bank active in the subprime market, was unable to roll over its paper in July and a rescue package was put together. On 9 August, BNP Paribas froze redemptions for three investment funds. On that day, the European Central Bank responded to the freezing up of the markets, and particularly the inter-bank market, by inject-ing almost €100 billion in overnight credit, and the US Federal Reserve followed suit quickly. By September, Northern Rock, which had financed its operations through a massive securiti-zation programme, was unable to secure finance and had to go to the Bank of England for liquidity.

So the crisis began as a liquidity squeeze, and the worst affected banks had a clear interest in presenting it that way, rather than acknowledging that they had made poor invest-ment and lending decisions. Some early analysis therefore centred on liquidity, and on its regulation. How was it that the banks could find themselves so short of liquidity in these circumstances? Were the liquidity requirements set by regulators inadequate?

One answer offered was that regulators had indeed focused far less attention on liquidity than on capital, over a long period. Attempts by the Basel Committee to agree on a global approach to liquidity in the 1980s failed. One of the most significant problems was the difficulty of agreeing the relative responsibilities of home and host regulators in a world of cross-border banking, and particularly in a crisis.[1] A consequence of this lack of an agreed regulatory framework was that banks ran down their stocks of liquid assets over a long period. Liquid assets are expensive for banks to hold as their return is low. In the 1950s, liquid assets typically accounted for around 30 per cent of a British clearing bank's total assets, largely in the form of treasury bills and short-dated government debt. More recently, cash holdings have averaged around 0.5 per cent of the balance sheet, and traditional liquid assets about 1 per cent of total liabilities.[2] Banks relied on central banks to provide liquidity in times of stress. As Charles Goodhart puts it, 'why should the banks bother with liquidity management when the central bank will do all that for them? The banks have been taking out a liquidity "put" on the central banks: they are in effect putting the downside of liquidity risk to the central bank.'[3]

Regulators understood this gap. In evidence to the UK Treasury Select Committee, Callum McCarthy, then Chairman of the Financial Services Authority, acknowledged 'an emphasis on capital as the fundamental measure and the relative neglect of liquidity'.[4] The Governor of the Bank of England said that the Bank had for a long time been very conscious of the absence of liquidity from the Basel Accords.[5]

How far can we accept this argument that the crisis was one of liquidity? Certainly the sharpest focus of the crisis in 2007 in Europe, and in 2008 on Wall Street, surrounded liquidity. In 2008, liquidity drained rapidly from the investment banks as clients took refuge in the lowest risk assets they could find. Bear Stearns had to be rescued because its cash ran out, falling by 90 per cent over three days. And after the collapse of Lehman Brothers, both Goldman Sachs and Morgan Stanley came within days of running out of cash. In those cases, fundamentally solvent institutions almost went under through a lack of liquidity. But Goodhart and Tsomocos note that 'concerns about liquidity and default interact. The original idea that the start of the financial crisis in August 2007 was just a liquidity problem, though a widely shared view at the time, was always ludicrous. Instead, the economic shock arising from the US housing market and its effect on mortgage-backed securities had both the prospect of a higher probability of default amongst an increasing range of banks and their associated conduits.'[6] In other words, those who withdrew liquidity from some of these troubled institutions were quite right to fear that their ultimate security was very weak.

But it is nonetheless arguable that the neglect of liquidity regulation was a significant contributory factor. And it was neglected at a time when, arguably, the changing nature of the banking system pointed to higher liquidity risk. Banks sought higher yields through increased leverage both on and off the balance sheet, and by investing in higher risk and complex structured instruments. The 'originate to distribute' market depended heavily on wholesale market funding. As Nigel Jenkinson, then of the Bank of England, said, 'banks' funding liquidity became increasingly dependent on sustained market liquidity. In advance of the crisis, high market confidence supported high market liquidity . . . but as leverage rose, credit spreads tightened, and liquidity risk premium narrowed, the likelihood of a sharpened pronounced correction continued to increase.'[7]

Brunnermeier[8] says it is useful to think of liquidity in two dimensions: funding liquidity and market liquidity. 'Funding liquidity describes the ease with which expert investors and arbitrageurs can obtain funding from (possibly less informed) financiers.' Traders use assets as collateral and borrow short-term against them, albeit with a haircut which must be financed by the trader's own capital. Many institutions came to depend heavily on short-term commercial paper or repo contracts to roll over their debt. But if funding liquidity is unavailable, banks may sell their positions instead, possibly at a loss, but not necessarily a catastrophic one. That is, of course, unless market liquidity is low at the same time. 'Market liquidity is low when selling the assets depresses the sale price and hence it becomes very costly to shrink the balance sheet. Market liquidity is equivalent to the relative ease of finding somebody who takes on the other side of the trade.' Brunnermeier summarizes the differences as: 'market liquidity refers to the transfer of the asset with its entire cash flow, while funding liquidity is like issuing debt, equity, or any other financial contract against the cash flow generated by an asset or trading strategy'. In the crisis of 2007–08, these two forms of liquidity interacted with each other in a toxic way. Through their interaction a relatively small shock can cause liquidity to dry up suddenly, generating sharp changes in asset prices and further escalating the crisis.

In these circumstances, either institutions fail, or the central bank steps in. Arguably, institutions which have allowed themselves to become excessively vulnerable to liquidity shocks do not deserve to survive. But the US authorities conducted an experiment in assessing the market consequences of permitting a large and interconnected investment bank to fail in September 2008. The consequences encouraged them to ensure that others did not follow Lehman Brothers into bankruptcy and other central banks around the world have taken a similar view. So, as Goodhart wittily puts it, 'just as it is the metier of God to have mercy on sinners, however heinous the sin, so it is the metier of central banks to provide liquidity to systemic financial institutions, however dubious are the assets on their balance sheets'.[9]

With the benefit of hindsight, we can see that banks which rely for their liquidity on selling or borrowing against assets which might fail to find a buyer were vulnerable to a crisis of confidence.[10] There is an argument, therefore, for strengthening their liquidity buffers. In extreme circumstances, when market confidence has evaporated, the financial authorities must step in. But there may be other times when temporary market breakdowns can be survived by institutions with larger cash reserves. Also, imposing more significant liquidity constraints on firms will make risky trading strategies more expensive and therefore constrain the build-up of risk in markets.

The Basel Committee has proposed a new global liquidity standard for internationally active banks, which would reverse the long decline in banks' liquidity holdings. There would be two components: a 'coverage' ratio, designed to ensure that banks have enough high quality liquid assets to survive through an 'acute stress scenario' lasting for a month, and the 'net stable funding' ratio, which aims to promote longer-term financing of assets and limits maturity mismatches (when funding is much more short-term than a bank's assets).[11] The maturity transformation role played by banks means that there is an inherent maturity mismatch at the heart of their balance sheets. But liquidity regulation can do something to prevent the extreme mismatches which were observed in the institutions which collapsed most quickly in the liquidity crisis of 2007.

Some regulators have already gone further. The Swiss have tripled the cash and cash equivalents they require their banks to hold. The FSA has proposed a rigorous new regime,[12] though it has given banks a lengthy transition period so as not to tighten quantitative standards before economic recovery is secured. The FSA regime will significantly tighten the definition of liquid assets, effectively to include only cash and short-dated government bonds. Some market participants are suspicious of this definition, on the grounds that it may be very convenient for a government with a very large funding requirement to require domestic financial institutions to hold its debt.

These measures appear logical, but they will be costly in the longer term. There is also an unresolved difficulty about the location of liquidity. The Lehman bankruptcy, when funds flowed out of London and into New York just before the firm's closure, demonstrated the risk to host regulators of allowing liquidity to flow freely through the branches of a firm with operations in many jurisdictions. National regimes, imposed country by country, will have the effect of obliging banks to hold more liquidity, in aggregate, than they would do were it to be managed centrally, adding further cost.

There are further conceptual difficulties to resolve. When is it permissible for a bank to use its liquidity cushion? Goodhart makes the point with the fable 'of the weary traveller who arrives at the station late at night and, to his delight, sees a taxi there who could take him to his distant destination. He hails the taxi, but the taxi driver replies that he cannot take him, since local bylaws require that there must always be one taxi driver standing at the station. Required liquidity is not true, usable liquidity.'[13] This causes Goodhart to believe that liquidity regulations should be couched in terms of general principles and not absolute minima. Others disagree, and believe that, without a legislated minimum, liquidity regulation is unlikely to be effective.

The imposition of liquidity requirements on individual firms may not be sufficient to respond to the types of strain which emerged in 2007. As Jenkinson puts it, 'good progress has been made in some areas, such as developing strong standards for liquidity risk management at individual banks that take account of system-wide stress. In other areas, such as calibrating the potential contribution of individual banks to potential system-wide liquidity strain, and reviewing how best to address spillovers and externalities from both the micro-prudential and macro-prudential perspective, research is just beginning.'[14] In part to respond to this systemic dimension some academics have proposed that banks should pay a kind of liquidity risk premium which would then give them access to central bank support at times of systemic crisis. But it is not clear how such a premium would be calculated, or indeed how entitlement to central bank support would be defined.

Most fundamentally, there remains no clear consensus as to whether the liquidity problem should be considered to be a symptom of the broader financial and economic crisis, or an underlying cause of it.

References

1. Liquidity Management. Charles Goodhart. Jackson Hole Symposium. Federal Reserve Bank of Kansas City. November 2009. www.kansascityfed.org
2. Pursuit of Profit has Led to Risky Lack of Liquidity. Tim Congdon. *Financial Times.* 10 September 2007. www.ft.com
3. Liquidity Risk Management. Charles Goodhart. Banque de France *Financial Stability Review* No. 11. February 2008. www.banque-france.fr

4. Oral Evidence Q127 – Banking Supervision and Regulation. Economic Affairs Committee. 10 February 2009. www.publications. parliament.uk/
5. Report on Banking Supervision and Regulation, Vol. I. Select Committee on Economic Affairs, House of Lords. 2 June 2009. www. publications.parliament.uk/
6. Liquidity, Default, and Market Regulation. Charles Goodhart and Dimitri Tsomocos. Vox. 12 November 2009. www.voxeu.org
7. Containing System-Wide Liquidity Risks: Some Issues and Challenges. Nigel Jenkinson. Speech at the University of Frankfurt Conference on the 'Law and Economics of Money and Finance in Times of Financial Crisis'. 15 May 2009.
8. Deciphering the Liquidity and Credit Crunch 2007–2008. Markus Brunnermeier. *Journal of Economic Perspectives*, Vol. 23, No. 1. Winter 2009.
9. Liquidity Management, Goodhart.
10. Fixing Regulation. Clive Briault. Centre for the Study of Financial Innovation. Report No. 91. October 2009. www.csfi.org.uk
11. International Framework for Liquidity Risk Measurement, Standards and Monitoring. Basel Committee on Banking Supervision. December 2009. www.bis.org
12. FSA Finalises Far-reaching Overhaul of UK Liquidity Regulation. Financial Services Authority. 5 October 2009. www.fsa.gov.uk/
13. Liquidity Risk Management, Goodhart.
14. Containing System-Wide Liquidity Risks, Jenkinson.

11

THE BLIND MAN AND THE ELEPHANT US REGULATION

The American financial regulatory system is quite unlike any other. Regulation is divided on essentially functional lines. There are several banking regulators, and subject to certain constraints banks are able to choose between them. National bodies include the Federal Reserve System (the Board and its regional banks), the Comptroller of the Currency and the Office of Thrift Supervision. There are also state-level banking supervisors, some of which, like the New York State Banking Department, are large and supervise banks with overseas branches. Cash securities and derivatives are handled by two separate agencies: state securities regulators, and state Attorney Generals who also have a role. There is no federal insurance regulator. Each state has an insurance commissioner. There is a separate deposit insurer, the FDIC, and a separate agency for the government-supported entities, Fannie Mae and Freddie Mac.

The system is byzantine and costly. There are far more people employed in financial regulation in the US, in relation to the size of its financial industry, than in any other developed country. Yet it was found seriously wanting in the crisis. Some argue that this complexity itself was an important reason for the failure, and that the multiplicity of agencies prevented the authorities building up a picture of the pressures in the system. How far can this contention be supported?

The complexities and weaknesses of the US system have been understood for some time. In the years before the crisis, several reports were produced, notably one by McKinsey & Company for the Mayor of New York and Senator Charles Schumer, drawing attention to the need for reform.[1] The motivation for this work was largely to enhance the competitiveness of New York as a financial centre at a time when it was believed that regulatory complexity was a disadvantage. The US system was regularly contrasted adversely with the attractive simplicity of the UK arrangement.

In response to these criticisms, the US Treasury began a project designed to promote reform and simplification. The financial crisis increased the urgency of this work, and a comprehensive set of reform proposals was published in March 2008.[2] That so-called 'blueprint' was outspokenly critical of the US regime. Paulson described the regulatory structure as 'hopelessly failed and outmoded and outdated'. The Treasury paper identified several particular flaws. It noted that 'a functional approach to regulation exhibits several inadequacies, the most significant being the fact that no single regulator possesses all of the information and authority necessary to monitor systemic risk'. Furthermore, 'jurisdictional disputes arise between and among the functional regulators'. A functional system 'also results in certain duplications of common activities across regulators'. The 2008 Treasury paper argued for far-reaching reform. In future there should be a market stability regulator, the Federal Reserve, a prudential financial regulator which pulls together the different banking supervisors, and a new federal charter for insurance companies. In parallel, there would be a new business conduct regulator, which would take on most aspects of the SEC's and the CFTC's responsibilities.

Others argued for even more fundamental change, taking the US system closer to the post-1997 UK model, with a US Financial Services Authority covering most of the responsibility of the existing patchwork of regulatory bodies.[3]

These proposals had made little headway when the crisis struck with full force during 2008. Since then, the debate on regulatory structure has become highly charged, with a wide range of proposals advanced by the administration, Senate and House of Representatives committees, the regulatory agencies themselves, the financial services industry and academics. Even though some elements of what is needed in a new system are agreed, by the early summer of 2010, no major reform programme had been implemented, in part reflecting the administration's difficulty in getting legislation through a highly fractious Congress.

In terms of regulatory structure, as opposed to the content and intensity of regulation, the principal arguments advanced for change were:

(1) That the crisis revealed the absence of a regulator able to take a comprehensive view of financial markets and to identify the emergence of systemic risk.
(2) The divisions between the SEC and the CFTC had made comprehensive regulation of securities and derivatives markets far more difficult to achieve, with costly consequences.
(3) Some systemically important institutions, like the major investment banks and AIG, lacked a consolidated supervisor able to take a view of the soundness of the institution as a whole.
(4) The AIG case highlighted the weaknesses of a state-based insurance regulation system.
(5) Competing banking supervisors, with banks able to 'charter shop' between them in search of the most congenial supervisor, had contributed to a weakening of prudential standards.
(6) There was a significant gap in terms of the enforcement of consumer protection.

The first point is broadly accepted, and reflects one of the recommendations in the earlier Paulson blueprint. But the question of who should undertake the systemic oversight role has proved controversial. The Federal Reserve might be thought to be the obvious candidate, but in the light of its performance in the run-up to the crisis, which many have strongly criticized, there has been considerable resistance to the idea that it should be rewarded with additional authority. So others have argued for a kind of council for systemic stability which would involve representatives of the other regulatory agencies and the US Treasury, or for a new national agency.

Although there is continued evidence of a dysfunctional relationship between the SEC and the CFTC (point (2)), there remains no consensus on merging the two agencies. In part, that reflects their different ancestry, with the CFTC seen as the 'Chicago regulator', while the SEC is the authority overseeing the New York markets. But the issue was complicated further by the dispute between the two on the regulation of derivatives, when the SEC took a more deregulatory approach than the CFTC. As a result, those who might in the past have been strongly in favour of consolidation in this area have been somewhat reticent to advance the case, and a merger is unlikely.

The third point, by contrast, is one on which a greater consensus has developed. Governor Daniel Tarullo of the Fed[4] has argued that there should be 'a statutory requirement for consolidated supervision of all systemically important financial firms – not just those affiliated with an insured bank'. The Obama Treasury under Tim Geithner has proposed 'new authority for the Federal Reserve to supervise all firms that could pose a threat to financial stability, even those that do not own banks',[5] which would in theory allow the Federal Reserve to regulate the parent of an insurance company, although the administration has not in fact proposed a new federal charter for potentially systemic insurance firms.

The lessons to be drawn from the expensive collapse of AIG are, however, much less clear. AIG's insurance operations were supervised by a range of state insurance regulators. But its losses occurred in its financial products area. Through its purchase of a savings and loans company in 1999, AIG was able to select as its primary regulator the Federal Office of Thrift Supervision (OTS), which was created after the savings and loans debacle of the 1980s. The OTS was AIG's consolidated supervisor under the Gramm-Leach-Bliley Act. The OTS also supervised both Indy Mac and Washington Mutual, both banks which effectively collapsed.

The OTS has acknowledged that it fell short in its oversight of AIG and 'did not sufficiently assess the susceptibility of highly illiquid, complex instruments' to ratings downgrades.[6]

The agency acknowledged that it showed supervisory weakness and did not take forceful action to curtail losses in AIG financial products from subprime and other non-traditional lending. Many have drawn the conclusion that had AIG had a Federal regulator overseeing the combined financial and insurance entities of the group, the enormously costly failure would have been prevented. It seemed absurd, particularly to overseas observers, that a group on the scale of AIG should have been regulated by a combination of the insurance regulator of one US state and the Office of Thrift Supervision.

Michael Powers of Temple University, Pennsylvania, describes the US system of insurance regulation as a 'nineteenth century institution charged with handling a twenty-first century financial services industry'.[7] A federal insurance regulator would in his view have been able to take charge of the oversight of AIG far more effectively, and could have forced the OTS to strengthen its oversight of the non-insurance parts of the group which brought it down. He recommends 'replacing America's archaic, cumbersome, and ineffective system of state insurance regulation with a modern federal agency'.

But the status quo has its defenders. Indeed, Eric Dinallo, the New York Insurance Superintendent, argued that 'what happened at AIG demonstrates the strength and effectiveness of state insurance regulation, not the opposite'.[8] An optional Federal charter for insurance companies would be wrong, in that 'when you permit companies to pick their regulator, you create the opportunity for regulatory arbitrage'. (In a way which is typical of the debate in the United States, he did not even contemplate the notion that there could be a single insurance regulator for the whole country.)

There is also no agreement on point (5). In the past, Alan Greenspan defended the diversity of the US system on the grounds that allowing banks to choose between a range of different regulators would keep those regulators 'honest', prevent them from putting burdensome obligations on their clients, and also promote innovation. Critics say that the ability of firms to choose their regulator in fact created a regulatory 'race to the bottom'. It is argued, for example, that 'when Countrywide Financial [a failed lender] felt pressure from federal agencies charged with overseeing it, executives of the giant mortgage lender simply switched regulators in the spring of 2007'.[9] Countrywide's new regulator, the OTS, 'promised more flexible oversight of issues related to the bank's mortgage lending'.[10] The then OTS Director, James Gilleran, had actively sought new companies to regulate, claiming 'our goal is to allow thrifts to operate with a wide breadth of freedom from regulatory intrusion'.[11] This seems a clear case of regulatory arbitrage.

But others contest this interpretation. A study in the *Journal of Money, Credit & Banking*[12] points out that in the decade from 1999 to 2008, 164 firms switched away from the OTS to another regulator, and only 119 switched to the OTS, representing a net loss of around $200 billion of assets under supervision. The OTS's loss of market share suggests that it was not the most competitive agency in terms of light regulatory requirements. It is argued, indeed, that 'those institutions at the very centre of the crisis had no say in the choice of their regulator'. Furthermore, 'other countries with consolidated supervision also experienced financial crisis'.[13] On this analysis, both the gaps in consolidated supervision and the choice of regulators were not material factors in creating or worsening the financial crisis.

There is no agreement, either, on the importance of stronger consumer protection through a consumer protection agency. The Obama administration maintains that 'multiple agencies have authority over consumer protection in financial products, but for historical reasons, the supervisory framework for enforcing those regulations had significant gaps and weaknesses'.[14] This gap was most visible in the mortgage market where, 'in the run-up to the financial crisis, mortgage companies and other firms outside the purview of bank regulation exploited that lack of clear accountability by selling mortgages and other products that were overly complicated and unsuited to borrowers' financial situation'.[15] The proposed remedy is the creation of a Consumer Financial Protection Agency (CFPA) with the authority and accountability to make sure that consumer protection regulations are written fairly and enforced vigorously. Such an agency should be able to fill in the gaps in the supervisory network.

But there has been much opposition in Congress to the

creation of a new agency. Some argue that it is an unnecessary additional tier of regulation, adding complexity to an already highly diversified system. Others, notably Joseph Stiglitz, argue that something more intrusive is needed, proposing a Financial Products Safety Commission which 'would assess the risks of particular products and determining their suitability for particular users'. The body would also look at the pricing of financial products.[16]

Overlaying these individual arguments is the broad question of whether a far simpler system would deliver at least the same benefits at lower cost. Both the Bush and Obama administrations have concluded that the logic of simplification is powerful, though neither have so far managed to overcome special pleading on the part of individual agencies and interest groups in Congress, in spite of the fact that much opinion in the financial industry itself favours simplification. The Financial Services Roundtable, which represents 100 large financial services firms, has argued that 'the chaotic system of financial regulation was a contributing factor to the current crisis'.[17] And former Secretary John Snow, using more vivid language, said, 'it's like the blind man and the elephant. They are all touching a piece of it, but they don't know what the big picture is.'[18]

But Larry White of New York University, while acknowledging that lax prudential regulation and inadequate consumer protection regulation explains much of the financial turmoil of 2008 and 2009, says that 'it is hard to claim that this regulatory laxity was due to the complexity of the US regulatory structure; equivalently, it is far from clear that a more unified and simplified regulatory structure would have prevented the crisis. For example, the more unified regulatory structures that exist in the United Kingdom and the rest of Western Europe have not been appreciably better at shielding their financial systems from the turmoil.'[19] He concludes that 'the cause of financial innovation, and even regulatory innovation, will be better served in a more diverse environment'.

Whoever is right, it would appear that, even though the crisis has caused two different US administrations to come out strongly in favour of structural reform, the forces resisting such reform remain powerful enough to prevent any radical legislation being enacted. US regulators will therefore need to continue to work within a highly complex environment, depending heavily on regulatory cooperation across legal frontiers, to allow them to piece together a picture of the elephant in their care.

References

1. Sustaining New York's and the US's Global Financial Services Leadership. McKinsey & Company Report commissioned by Mayor Michael Bloomberg and Senator Charles Schumer. 2007. www.nyc.gov
2. Blueprint for a Modernized Financial Regulatory Structure. US Department of Treasury. 31 March 2008. www.treas.gov
3. A Pragmatic Approach to the Phased Consolidation of Financial Regulation in the United States. Howell Jackson. Harvard Law School Public Law Research Paper No. 09–19. November 2008. www.law.harvard.edu
4. Financial Regulation in the Wake of the Crisis. Governor Daniel Tarullo. Speech at the Peterson Institute for International Economics, Washington, DC. 8 June 2009. www.federalreserve.gov
5. Financial Regulatory Reform – A New Foundation: Rebuilding Financial Supervision and Regulation. US Department of Treasury. 17 June 2009. www.treas.gov
6. An Examination of What Went Wrong with American International Group. Statement of Scott Poliakoff before the Committee on Banking, Housing and Urban Affairs of the US Senate. 5 March 2009. www.banking.senate.gov
7. Insurance Regulation in America – Playing Out of its League. Michael Powers. *Journal of Risk Finance*, Vol. 10, No. 1. 2009. http://emeraldinsight.com
8. Testimony by New York Superintendent Eric Dinallo before the Committee on Banking, Housing and Urban Affairs of the US Senate. 5 March 2009. www.banking.senate.gov
9. Banking Regulator Played Advocate Over Enforcer. Binyamin Appelbaum and Ellen Nakashima. *The Washington Post*. 23 November 2008. www.washingtonpost.com
10. Ibid.
11. Ibid.
12. Is Three a Crowd? Competition Among Regulators in Banking. Richard Rosen. *Journal of Money, Credit and Banking*, Vol. 35, No. 6. December 2003.
13. Would Consolidating Regulators Avoid the Next Crisis? Mark Calabria. FinReg21. 17 November 2009. www.finreg21.com

14. Financial Regulatory Reform, US Department of Treasury.
15. Ibid.
16. The Future of Financial Services Regulation – Testimony of Joseph Stiglitz. US House of Representatives' Committee on Financial Services. 21 October 2008. www.house.gov
17. Regulation of Systemic Risk – Hearing of Steve Bartlett. US House of Representatives' Committee on Financial Services. 17 March 2009. www.house.gov
18. The Role of Federal Regulators and the Financial Crisis – Hearing of John Snow. US House of Representatives' Committee on Oversight and Government Reform. 23 October 2008. www.house.gov
19. US Financial Regulation: A Hopeless Tangle, or Complexity for a Purpose? Lawrence White. QFinance Best Practice. 2009. www.qfinance.com

12

SEC – RIP?

The Securities and Exchange Commission (SEC) was the consolidated supervisor of the five major independent investment banks at the beginning of the crisis. During the course of 2008, one of them, Lehman Brothers, went into bankruptcy, while two others, Bear Stearns and Merrill Lynch, were effectively rescued – the first with explicit Federal Reserve support – by JP Morgan and Bank of America. For an agency to lose 20 per cent of its supervised universe might be regarded as unfortunate, to lose 60 per cent suggests carelessness or worse.

The SEC was a reluctant consolidated supervisor. It is commonly argued that there is a significant cultural difference between banking supervisors and securities regulators. The former are thought to have the mindset of the doctor, focused first on attempting to cure the patient when a problem emerges, and only subsequently seeking to identify the causes of the failure and the individuals responsible. They are often slow to censure. This mindset arises from the belief that the failure of a bank can generate significant collateral damage and injure innocent bystanders. So failure must be regarded as the last resort, and enforcement action can precipitate the collapse the regulator is trying to forestall.

The SEC, by contrast, is in the 'cop' model of regulators. It talks of itself as a guardian of investor interests, keen to take enforcement action where necessary, without consideration for the viability and stability of the firms being prosecuted. In relation to small brokers and asset managers, this assumption makes little difference. They are unlikely to generate systemic risk, even in the event of complete failure. But as the investment banks grew larger and larger, and took on central roles in many traded markets, with highly complex inter-linkages with other financial institutions around the globe, it became anachronistic to ignore the potential for systemic risk. Yet the view taken of the risk of failure of these institutions by the SEC, when challenged by foreign regulators, was that the investment banks were fundamentally different from commercial banks. If they ran into difficulty, they would wind down both sides of their balance sheets, leaving a small net positive or negative balance at the end of the process. Then the job of the regulator would be to oversee an orderly liquidation, and turn out the lights.

Banking regulators did not accept this assumption. They could see that the investment banks were central to many markets in the US and overseas. The lack of a regulator of their parent, overseeing its prudential soundness, was increasingly seen as a glaring omission. In Europe there was strong political pressure for consolidated supervision of the investment banks, who were playing more and more important roles in European financial markets. The point was raised in the Financial Stability Forum. There was also a competitive dimension, in that the capital rules which applied to their universal bank competitors in Europe were not imposed on the US institutions.

After lengthy international debates, the European Union decided to legislate, and passed the Financial Groups Directive in 2002. That Directive required all financial institutions operating in EU markets to have a consolidated supervisor, responsible for the capital position and overall financial integrity of the firm. If there was no consolidated supervisor at group level, then the firm would be required to sub-consolidate its European entities and hold capital in Europe at that level.

The latter option was potentially costly and capital-inefficient for the investment banks. Their European capital would be trapped, and could not then be used to back other parts of the business. Some therefore considered locating their headquarters in Europe to take advantage of consolidated supervision there. The prospect of supervision by the FSA seemed attractive to some. But, eventually, the US authorities decided to respond. After a failed attempt by the Office of Thrift Supervision to offer itself as the consolidated supervisor of the major investment banks, the SEC constructed a programme of consolidated supervision which met the terms of the European Directive. Investment banks could become, in the SEC's terminology, 'consolidated supervised entities'. The SEC already regulated the broker dealer subsidiaries of the investment banks, but this gave it some purchase on the parent holding company. Technically the programme was voluntary, but the five main investment banks opted into it in 2004.

The task of consolidated supervision proved difficult for the SEC. Their staff had little understanding of, or training for, the role. Different divisions of the SEC took different approaches and did not communicate well with each other. They did not behave as banking supervisors now do, with regular meetings with boards of directors and audit committees. The SEC applied a version of Basel II, but firms were nonetheless allowed to increase their leverage substantially. The leverage ratio of Lehman Brothers went from 22.7 to 29.7 times its capital during the period of 2003–2006[1] while Bear Stearns' leverage ratio went from 27.4 in 2003 to 32.5 in 2007[2] and to more than 35 in March 2008.[3] When the crisis hit, it became clear that the entities, particularly those two, did not have adequate capital or liquidity to withstand the market pressures. Their failure, therefore, led to a wave of criticism of the supervisory performance of the SEC, under its then Chairman, former Republican Congressman Christopher Cox.

The highest profile critic was the Republican Presidential candidate John McCain, who said 'the Chairman of the SEC serves at the appointment of the President and has betrayed the public's trust. If I were President today, I would fire him.'[4] Douglas Holtz-Eakin, a former head of the Congressional Budget Office and an adviser to McCain, noted 'the surveillance would appear to be severely impaired because we're having entities show up every day that are in desperate shape without any warning'.[5] John Coffee, a Columbia University securities law professor, noted 'if 60% of the investment banks of any size have disappeared, I can't say the SEC is as good at prudential financial regulation as they are at disclosure and consumer regulation'.[6]

The SEC's own Inspector General, David Kotz, was asked by the Senate to examine the firm's regulation of Bear Stearns. The Inspector General's reports were highly critical. It concluded bluntly that the SEC 'failed to carry out its mission in the oversight of Bear Stearns'.[7] The SEC took no action as Bear Stearns provided more collateral to lenders and regulators did not formally, or informally, pressure the firm to raise capital.

In September 2008, after the Lehman Brothers failure, the SEC programme was formally shut down. Apart from the two failures, Merrill Lynch had been taken over, and the Federal Reserve instructed both Morgan Stanley and Goldman Sachs to convert themselves into bank holding companies subject to its supervision. In announcing the closure of the programme, Chairman Cox said 'the last six months have made it abundantly clear that voluntary regulation does not work'[8] and that 'the fact that investment bank holding companies could withdraw from this voluntary supervision at their discretion diminished the perceived mandate'[9] of the SEC programme, and weakened its effectiveness.

This argument was not found universally persuasive. While it was technically true that the programme was voluntary, in that it was not mandated by US law, the five investment banks needed SEC regulation to meet the terms of the EU Directive without expensive sub-consolidation in Europe. Furthermore, in 2007 the then SEC Commissioner Annette Nazareth said, 'the aim is to effectively monitor the holding company, and unregulated entities within the group, for financial and operational weaknesses that might place regulated entities or the broader financial system at risk. The Commission has authority under these rules to take action in the event of a weakness or potential weakness.'[10] And it was argued that in practice, an SEC Chairman could have imposed his will on holding companies had he so wished.

Former SEC Chairmen offered a partial defence of the regulator's role. Harvey Pitt said 'the one thing that's clear is that the SEC didn't cause these problems' and blamed the structure of financial regulation in the US which left the SEC and other regulators without the tools to regulate new markets. 'In essence what we have is a 21st century financial system, and a 19th century regulatory system,'[5] he said. Richard Breeden, another former Chairman, while noting that 'we will have to re-examine how permissive [the agency] had been', argued that there were other factors at work and that the SEC could not be seen to be solely responsible for the increase in leverage.[11]

Whatever the merits of these arguments in mitigation, it would seem that the SEC's brief history as a prudential regulator is over. In the extensive debates on the future of the US regulatory system through 2009–2010, there were no advocates of a return to consolidated supervision by the SEC, or a renewed role for it in either prudential or systemic oversight. The Commission undoubtedly lost prestige and status as a result. The Madoff and Stanford cases, though not central to the crisis, were further blows.

References

1. Lehman Brothers Annual Report 2007. www.lehman.com/
2. Bear Stearns Annual Report 2003 and 2007. www.bearstearns.com/
3. The Last Days of Bear Stearns. Roddy Boyd. 31 March 2008. Fortune. http://money.cnn.com/
4. McCain's Scapegoat. *The Wall Street Journal.* 19 September 2008. http://online.wsj.com/
5. SEC's Cox Catches Blame for Financial Crisis. Theo Francis. *Business Week.* 19 September 2008. www.businessweek.com
6. Ibid.
7. Cox's SEC Censors Report on Bear Stearns Collapse. Mark Pittman, Elliot Blair Smith and Jesse Westbrook. 7 October 2008. www.bloomberg.com
8. Cox ends CSE program; SEC's Inspector General Criticizes SEC Oversight of Bear Stearns. Barbara Black. 28 September 2008. http://lawprofessors.typepad.com/securities/
9. Report Says SEC Failed in Oversight of Bear Stearns. Cecilia Kang. *The Washington Post.* 27 September 2008. www.washingtonpost.com
10. SEC's Cox Catches Blame, Francis.
11. Ibid.

13

FINANCIAL WEAPONS OF MASS DESTRUCTION DERIVATIVES

As we have seen, the system of financial regulation in the United States is unusual in many respects. One feature is unique. There are two separate agencies regulating cash securities and derivatives. The SEC regulates cash equities while the Commodities Futures Trading Commission (CFTC) regulates the futures and options markets. The predecessors of the CFTC were principally focused on regulating commodities markets. But when futures and options contracts developed in the financial markets, scope for regulatory overlap and awkward borderlines emerged. Regulatory turf wars between the two agencies have broken out at regular intervals over the past thirty-five years.

A particular dispute arose in the late 1990s, one which has acquired some significance in the crisis. The then Chair of the CFTC, Brooksley Born, came into conflict with the other members of the President's Working Group on Financial Markets: Robert Rubin, the Treasury Secretary (later Larry Summers); Alan Greenspan of the Federal Reserve; and Arthur Levitt of the SEC. The SEC issued a proposal to bring securities activities conducted outside the regulated broker dealer affiliates of securities firms into broker dealer supervision, through a relaxation of net capital and other rules for Over-The-Counter (OTC) derivatives dealers. This proposal was known as 'Broker Dealer Lite'. In response, the CFTC issued a concept release, asking for comments on the regulation of the over-the-counter derivatives market, which pointed to a new regulatory approach under the CFTC's aegis.

The other members of the President's Working Group on Financial Markets immediately asked Congress to prevent the CFTC from changing its existing treatment of OTC derivatives. At the time, the dispute was presented as jurisdictional. But there was a more fundamental disagreement about whether close regulation of these markets was justified or not. The other members of the President's Working Group believed that 'there is no compelling evidence of problems involving bilateral swap agreements that would warrant regulation under the Commodity Exchange Act (CEA)'.[1] Brooksley Born, however, believed that the case for regulation was made out. She saw the potential for risks which might destabilize firms and markets.

There was extensive Wall Street lobbying against the CFTC proposal. In the event, Born was overruled and Congress passed a law preventing the CFTC from changing its treatment of OTC derivatives. She resigned in June 1999 and, although the Long-Term Capital Management affair caused some concerns about the potential for systemic risk generated by derivatives transactions, the Commodity Futures Modernization Act 2000 excluded transactions in financial derivatives from the purview of the CEA. So-called 'eligible contract participants' could enter into transactions on or off electronic trading facilities without being subject to any of the regulatory oversight applicable to futures.

This somewhat arcane dispute, which interested other financial regulators at the time, but few other people, acquired a special significance in 2007–08.

Some financiers had drawn attention to the risks inherent in financial derivatives. George Soros had noted that he avoided using derivative contracts 'because we don't really understand how they work'.[2] Warren Buffet described them as 'financial weapons of mass destruction, carrying dangers which, while now latent, are potentially lethal'.[3] On the other side of the argument, Alan Greenspan told the Senate Banking Committee in 2003 that 'what we have found over the years in the marketplace is that derivatives have been an extraordinarily useful vehicle to transfer risk from those who shouldn't be taking it, to those who are willing, and capable, of doing so'.[4] He thought it would be a mistake to regulate these contracts more intensively.

Brooksley Born had argued in Congressional testimony in the late 1990s that trading in derivatives, if not subject to transparency rules, could 'threaten our regulated markets, or indeed our economy, without any Federal Agency knowing about it'.[5] Her proposed remedy was greater disclosure of trades and the establishment of capital reserves to provide a cushion against losses. Although the other regulators at the time did not agree, Robert Rubin has subsequently said that he privately favoured regulating derivatives, but 'all of the forces in the system were arrayed against it, the industry certainly didn't want any increase in these requirements. There was no potential for mobilizing public opinion.'[6] Arthur Levitt, then Chair of the SEC, says he now regrets the decision to oppose regulation. 'I think it is fair to say that regulators should have considered the implications . . . of the exploding derivatives markets.'[7]

Born has subsequently justified the view she took at the time, 'I think the markets grew so enormously with so little oversight or regulation, that it made the financial crisis much deeper and more pervasive than it otherwise might have been.'[8] Frank Partnoy, a former Morgan Stanley investment banker now a professor of law in San Diego, argues 'history already has shown that Greenspan was wrong about virtually everything and Brooksley was right, I think she has been entirely vindicated . . . if there is one person we should have listened to, it was Brooksley.'[9]

By 2009, the Chairs of both the SEC and the CFTC had achieved a common position. In May 2009, Mary Schapiro, the new Obama-appointed Chair of the SEC, said 'current Federal statutes significantly restrict the ability of financial regulators to obtain reporting or record keeping in the OTC derivatives market . . . in addition, central clearing for credit default swaps and other OTC derivatives would bring to this market much needed transparency.'[10] Acting CFTC Chairman Michael Dunn said, 'by regulating these contracts and having the ability to set position limits, we will have the ability and necessary information to ensure market integrity'.[11] Subsequently, the Obama administration proposed detailed legislation regulating the OTC derivatives markets to promote transparency and efficiency, and to guard against excessive risk. Once again, many on Wall Street opposed it.

How significant was the 2000 legislation, and the rejection of the CFTC proposal? James Hamilton, of the Federal Securities Law Reporter, argues that 'this lack of regulation led to disastrous consequences. Many institutions and investors had substantial positions in credit default swaps, swaps tied to asset-backed securities, complex instruments whose risk characteristics proved to be poorly understood even by the most sophisticated of market participants. At the same time, excessive risk-taking and poor counter-party risk management by many banks saddled the financial system with an enormous unrecognized level of risk . . . lacking authority to regulate the OTC derivatives market, regulators were unable to identify or mitigate the enormous systemic threat that had developed.'[12]

The case for some regulation of these markets is now quite widely accepted, though perhaps not by Alan Greenspan, who in his 2007 memoir, *The Age of Turbulence,* wrote 'it seems superfluous to constrain trading in some of the newer derivatives and other innovative financial contracts of the past decade. The worst have failed; investors no longer fund them and are not likely to in the future.'[13]

It remains uncertain how far a regulatory regime based on transparency, as proposed by the CFTC Chair in 1998, would have prevented the build-up of risk seen in 2003–2007. But one important feature of the crisis was the difficulty of identifying where risks and losses lay in the financial system, which in turn created some of the uncertainty behind the liquidity crisis of 2007. Greater visibility of the location of market risks, and the standardization of contracts that bringing derivatives on exchange would have been likely to engender, would probably have helped the authorities to manage the crisis at that time. It is probable that regulatory reform in the US will improve on-exchange trading, and greater transparency.

References

1. Over-the-Counter Derivatives Markets and the Commodity Exchange Act – Report of The President's Working Group on Financial Markets. November 1999. www.ustreas.gov/
2. The Reckoning – Taking Hard New Look at Greenspan Legacy. Peter Goodman. *The New York Times*. 9 October 2008. www.nytimes.com
3. Ibid.
4. Hearing of Alan Greenspan before the Committee on Banking, Housing and Urban Affairs of the US Senate. 16 July 2003. www.banking.senate.gov
5. Testimony of Brooksley Born on Long-Term Capital Management before the US House of Representatives – Committee on Banking and Financial Services. 1 October 1998.
6. Brooksley Born and Alan Greenspan. Jon Mandle. Crooked Timber. 9 October 2008. www.crookedtimber.org
7. Prophet and Loss. Rick Schmitt. *Stanford Magazine*. March/April 2009. www.stanfordalumni.org
8. Brooksley Born and Alan Greenspan, Mandle.
9. Ibid.
10. Speech by Mary Schapiro at the Joint Press Conference on OTC Derivatives Regulation, held at the Department of The Treasury on 13 May 2009. www.sec.gov/
11. Speech by Michael Dunn at the Joint Press Conference on OTC Derivatives Regulation, held at the Department of The Treasury on 13 May 2009. www.cftc.gov/
12. Administration Unveils Legislation to Regulate Derivatives, Including Credit Default Swaps. James Hamilton. 11 August 2009. www.financialcrisisupdate.com
13. *The Age of Turbulence: Adventures in a New World*. Alan Greenspan. Penguin Press. 2007.

14

FEDERAL MORTGAGE REGULATION

The financial crisis began in the US subprime mortgage market. That market grew in size from almost zero in the early 1990s to a total of new origination of $625 billion in 2005. The growth occurred largely among borrowers in lower-income households, who could not secure conventional mortgage credit. The market relied on rising house prices, as many mortgagees remortgaged during the life of the loans in order to continue to make payments. The market was rife with bad practices: high and repeated commissions, predatory lending, etc. When house prices stopped rising at the end of 2006, the market began to unravel with rapidly rising default and repossession rates, and many mortgage lenders went bankrupt.

How could this market have been allowed to develop in the way it did, without intervention from any of the many regulators in the United States? Many of the lenders were not in practice regulated, and nor were the mortgage brokers themselves. It has been argued that the Federal Reserve was in a position to step into the market, yet failed to do so. Henry Waxman, the Chairman of the Committee on Oversight and Government Reform in the US House of Representatives, said 'the Federal Reserve had the authority to stop the irresponsible lending practices that fuelled the subprime mortgage market. But its long-time Chairman, Alan Greenspan, rejected pleas that he intervene.'[1]

Specifically, the Fed could have investigated lenders affiliated with national banks. Press reports suggest that Ned Gramlich, a Federal Reserve Governor who died in 2007, had argued within the Federal Reserve for such oversight, but had been rebuffed by Greenspan. Housing advocacy groups made representations to the Federal Reserve and pressed for a voluntary code of conduct. The Chief Executive of the Center for Responsible Lending in North Carolina said 'the Federal Reserve could have stopped this problem dead in its tracks, if the Fed had done its job we would not have had the abusive lending and we would not have a foreclosure crisis in virtually every community across America'.[2]

Gramlich drew attention to the rapid growth in the market and the potential problems which that growth could produce, notably in a speech in Chicago in 2004.[3] He noted 'the relatively high delinquency rate in the subprime to raise issues' and pointed to the regulatory gaps: 'we still have no obvious way to monitor the lending behaviour of independent mortgage companies'.

Sheila Bair, the Chair of the FDIC, has been more outspoken in her criticisms of the Fed. 'Hindsight is always 20–20, but it's clear the Fed should have acted earlier.' She developed this critique in a statement to the Financial Crisis Inquiry Commission in January 2010.[4] In that testimony she drew attention to the Home Ownership and Equity Protection Act (HOEPA), which is part of the Truth in Lending Act. Regulations under both Acts are the responsibility of the Board of Governors of the Federal Reserve and apply to both bank and non-bank lenders. A report by the Department of Housing & Urban Development and the Treasury in 2000, entitled 'Curbing Predatory Home Mortgage Lending', found that certain terms of subprime loans were harmful or abusive and the Federal Reserve should use its authority to prohibit abusive practices. In 2001, the Fed did issue a rule that addressed a narrow range of predatory lending but, as Bair argues, 'it was not until 2008 that the Federal Reserve issued a more extensive regulation using its HOEPA authority to restrict unfair, deceptive or abusive practices in the mortgage market'. She argued that 'if HOEPA regulations had been amended in 2001, instead of 2008, a large number of the toxic mortgage loans could not have originated and much of the crisis may have been prevented'.

Alan Greenspan does not accept this criticism, arguing that the Fed was poorly equipped to investigate deceptive lending, and that it was not to blame for the housing bubble and bust.[5] He has also argued that the subprime mortgage market did bring the benefits of home ownership to a broader range of American citizens.

It is not clear whether Federal Reserve examinations of affiliates of national banks would have prevented the abuses in the subprime market. The Fed has now, however, accepted that it should assert its ability to oversee mortgage lending affiliates of national banks. But the subprime market has not restarted on any significant scale, so the appropriateness and effectiveness of its regulatory powers have not been established.

References

1. The Role of Federal Regulators and the Financial Crisis. US House of Representatives' Committee on Oversight and Government Reform. 23 October 2008. www.house.gov
2. Fed Shrugged as Subprime Crisis Spread. Edmund Andrews. *The New York Times*. 18 December 2007. www.nytimes.com
3. Subprime Mortgage Lending: Benefits, Costs, and Challenges. Edward M. Gramlich. Speech at the Financial Services Roundtable. Chicago. 21 May 2004. www.federalreserve.gov
4. Statement of Sheila Bair before the Financial Crisis Inquiry Commission. Washington, DC. 14 January 2010. www.fcic.gov
5. *The Age of Turbulence*. Alan Greenspan. Penguin Press. 2007.

15

CASINO BANKING: THE END OF GLASS-STEAGALL

After the Wall Street crash the US Congress passed, in 1933, the Glass-Steagall Act which banned commercial banks from underwriting securities, forcing banks to choose between being a simple lender or becoming an underwriter, or what came to be known as a broker dealer. One very visible consequence was the split of the House of Morgan into the commercial bank, JP Morgan and the broker dealer Morgan Stanley. Some countries, including Japan, followed this model. Others, notably in continental Europe, did not.

From the 1960s onwards, attempts were made to find ways around Glass-Steagall prohibitions, or to amend them. One significant amendment occurred in the spring of 1987, when the Federal Reserve Board voted three to two in favour of easing the restrictions, in spite of the opposition of then Chairman Paul Volcker. Following Alan Greenspan's appointment in the summer of 1987, further softening of the impact of Glass-Steagall was engineered by the Federal Reserve, which is thought to have given tacit support to Sandy Weill, who in the late 1990s engineered the construction of a financial hypermarket when Citibank, Salomon Brothers and Travellers Insurance Group merged. This merger anticipated the repeal of Glass-Steagall which occurred in late 1999, when Congress passed the Financial Services Modernization Act, also known as the Gramm-Leach-Bliley Act.

There were those, including Paul Volcker, who feared the consequences of repeal at the time. For them, the financial crisis brought confirmations of their worst fears when the Federal Reserve converted the remaining investment banks into financial holding companies with access to Fed funds at attractive rates. In the aftermath of the failure of Lehman Brothers, both Goldman Sachs and Morgan Stanley were converted, over a weekend. This move, which raised the spectre of US taxpayers being called upon to bail out Goldman Sachs, reignited a long running debate about what to do with 'too big to fail' firms and how to insulate insured deposits from the risks inherent in what was increasingly known as 'casino banking'.

The Group of Thirty published a report, in early 2009, from a group co-chaired by Paul Volcker. In it, Volcker and others argued for a form of separation of commercial and investment banking.[1] Specifically, he argued that banks should not be allowed to own, invest in or sponsor hedge funds or private equity funds or engage in proprietary trading operations for their own profit, unrelated to serving their customers. This suggestion, a year later, became a specific proposal by the Obama administration, known as the 'Volcker rule', often dubbed Glass-Steagall-Lite, as it encapsulates roughly the spirit of the old legislation, if not the precise terms of the 1933 Act. Other influential voices, notably Mervyn King, the Governor of the Bank of England, have supported the idea in general terms. A version of the rule has appeared in Senator Dodd's Bill. European governments, including the British, have broadly been opposed to a legislated split of this kind, which would have significant implications for European universal banks like Deutsche Bank or BNP Paribas.

Was the repeal of Glass-Steagall an important contributor to the crisis? The argument in favour has some theoretical attractions, and the prospect of risk-seeking investment banks benefiting from the Fed's safety net certainly gives pause for thought. But the case for the Financial Modernization Act being the root cause of the crisis is strongly contested. Randy Kroszner, a former Fed governor now a professor of economics at the University of Chicago, argues that 'the experience of the last few years, however, does not provide strong support for such an argument. In the US, for example, the interconnected problems arose not primarily from the mixing of commercial and investment banking at individual institutions. Bear Stearns, Merrill Lynch, and Lehman Brothers were not commercial bank holding companies and so their troubles had nothing to do with allowing commercial and investment banking to occur in the same holding company.'[2] He goes on to argue that the Volcker rule 'would likely result in greater fragmentation of the financial system, with the likely consequence of increasing rather than decreasing interconnectedness of banking institutions' funding sources to other financial institutions and markets'. Professor Lawrence White of NYU takes a similar view: 'the frenzy of mortgage originations and securitizations that lay at the core of the debacle . . . could have and would have proceeded in much the same fashion even if Glass-Steagall had not been repealed in 1999.'[3]

On the European side, Hans-Werner Sinn notes that 'if Obama succeeds in anchoring a separation of commercial and investment banks worldwide at the G20 negotiations, this would mean a destruction of the European banking world . . . crisis prevention will certainly not come from a return to a system of bank separation . . . moreover, it is doubtful whether the likelihood of government rescue will really be reduced. The State will have to rescue large investment banks even if they do not manage customer savings, since no one would accept a repeat of the Lehman Brothers disaster.'[4]

Adair Turner, in his review of the crisis, was also not attracted to a Glass-Steagall separation, arguing that a preferable approach is to strengthen capital reserves, and ensure some ring fencing of capital to back particular activities. Specifically, he argues for a very significant increase, perhaps a tripling, of the capital banks must hold in their trading books.[5] Turner and others have also noted the difficulty of establishing a clear separation between proprietary and non-proprietary activities, and the artificiality of the restrictions which would arise from so doing. If customers want to hedge their positions in foreign exchange or interest rates, should they be forbidden from doing that with their bank? An investment bank might reasonably wish to short a stock similar to a company whose IPO they are managing. If their underwriting leaves them with unsold stock, can they maintain that short position? When does hedging become proprietary trading?

Mervyn King is not impressed with this line of argument. He argues that it is hard to see why a separation is impractical, and believes that those who argue against separation have a less realistic view. 'Anyone who proposed giving government guarantees to retail depositors and other creditors, and then suggested that such funding could be used to finance highly risky and speculative activities, would be thought rather unworldly.'[6]

An alternative argument is that while a rigid Glass-Steagall-like separation would undoubtedly cause a major restructuring of the banking system, the Volcker rule might have only a modest impact. It would prevent investments in hedge funds by investment banks, but that has been a very small part of their activities. The same is true of private equity, though perhaps Goldman Sachs might be more affected by such a prohibition than others. Only if a very broad definition of what is proprietary trading were developed, and investment banks were excluded from that activity altogether, would it have a great deal of impact on them. On this argument, the Volcker rule – which in the early summer of 2010 seemed likely to be legislated in the US – would not be a very significant reform. Furthermore, the problem of institutions which are too interconnected, and therefore systemic, to be allowed to fail, yet which are not engaging in money transmission or retail deposit-taking activities, where the public policy case for government backing is strong, would remain. So Glass-Steagall-Lite is not an effective solution to the 'too big to fail' problem. As Martin Wolf says, 'in this crisis, at least, banks' investments and hedge funds, private equity and even proprietary trading were simply not the core of what went wrong'.[7]

References

1. Financial Reform – A Framework for Financial Stability. Working Group on Financial Reform. Group of Thirty. January 2009. www.group30.org
2. Interconnectedness, Fragility and the Financial Crisis. Randall

Kroszner. Financial Crisis Inquiry Commission. Washington, DC. 26 February 2010. www.fcic.gov

3. Lessons from the Debacle of '07–'08 for Financial Regulation and Its Overhaul. Lawrence White. Unpublished paper. December 2008.

4. A new Glass-Steagall Act? Hans-Werner Sinn. 4 March 2010. www.voxeu.org

5. The Turner Review: A Regulatory Response to the Global Banking Crisis. Financial Services Authority. March 2009. www.fsa.gov.uk

6. Speech to Scottish business organizations. Mervyn King. 20 October 2009. www.bankofengland.co.uk

7. Volcker's Axe is Not Enough to Cut Banks to Size. Martin Wolf. *The Financial Times*. 26 January 2010. www.ft.com

16

TOO BIG TO FAIL

During the crisis, several governments found themselves required to rescue large banks. That is the case in the US and the UK, where banks like Royal Bank of Scotland and Citigroup were effectively taken over by the state, and also in Ireland, the Netherlands and elsewhere. These rescues were, at least in the short term, highly costly to governments. They were also hard to defend to taxpayers. Why were governments prepared to rescue banks, run by conspicuously well-paid and often unappealing individuals, when they were not prepared to extend some of their support to struggling manufacturers? (In the US, the major car manufacturers were similarly rescued, but other companies were allowed to go to the wall.) The case was easier to defend where large sums of deposits by retail customers were at risk. But what about institutions like Lehman Brothers? Of course the US government famously did not rescue Lehman, but the dramatic market consequences of allowing it to fail showed that investment banks had become 'systemic'. So after the Lehman collapse, Morgan Stanley and Goldman Sachs were also supported by the Federal Reserve and took TARP (Troubled Assets Relief Programme) funds from the US Treasury.

In some cases there may eventually be no net cost to the taxpayer from such support. In the US, the TARP funds were quickly repaid by Morgan Stanley and Goldman Sachs, at a healthy return for the government. In other cases, where the government still owns shares (as in RBS, for example) it is still not clear what the final net cost will be. That will depend on the government's skill in managing its exit. But it is likely that, overall, there will be a net cost to the taxpayer from these support operations, and the broader economic impact of the crisis has been very expensive for the Exchequer, in countries with large financial systems.

As a result, much attention has been focused on the 'too big to fail' question. It is argued that large banks face a fundamental asymmetry of incentives. Banks which benefit from an explicit state guarantee, whether simply in the form of insured deposits, or through the availability of lender of last resort support in a crisis, face a situation in which where they take on more risk, they are likely to earn higher rewards, in the good times. Those rewards will accrue partly to shareholders, but mostly to managers, many of whom have become incontinently wealthy in recent years. Yet when the markets turn down severely, the taxpayer is obliged to step in to maintain the integrity of the firm. So it is 'heads the bankers win, tails the taxpayers lose'. Banks do not face the essential risk of collapse, which ought to impose some discipline on their risk appetite.

How far does this incentive structure explain the behaviour which led to the crisis? Undoubtedly, the theory is powerful. Within firms, there have certainly been examples of highly risky trading strategies which rewarded individuals in the short run, while imposing long-term costs on the firm as a whole. But at the level of the whole institution, bankers argue that they do not think in that way. Their aim is to stay in business indefinitely. It is not possible to find a smoking gun which proves the theory, in the form of an internal memorandum to traders saying 'never mind the risk, boys, if it all goes wrong the government will bail us out'.

Bankers would also argue that the high reputational cost to them of failure is a strong constraining factor, and that their overriding objective is the maximization of shareholder value. In crises shareholders lose catastrophically. But one counter to that argument is that while the theology of bank rescues, for example as set out by Eddie George, the former governor of the Bank of England in 1993, holds that 'in a rescued bank the shareholders should lose everything and the depositors nothing',[1] in practice that proved hard to engineer. Central banks and governments lacked effective resolution mechanisms which allowed them to take over a failing institution, wipe out the shareholders, and re-establish it.

Following these arguments, governments and regulators have tried to find ways of realigning incentives to prevent institutions being in a position effectively to blackmail governments to support them. Some of the potential remedies are, in principle, relatively uncontroversial, like the establishment of a resolution authority, and the requirement on potentially systemic institutions to produce 'living wills', in other words to explain how they would wind themselves down in the event of a further crisis. (The main aim of those wills would be to prevent the bank getting into a position of such vulnerability in the first place.) But they are complex in practice, and banks argue that knowledge of a competitor's living will would be very helpful in, for example, a takeover.

The lack of a clear mechanism for handling the failure of a large complex financial institution (LCFI) like Lehman Brothers made the crisis harder to manage. As Treasury Secretary Tim Geithner pointed out in 2009, 'The US government does not have the legal means today to manage the orderly restructuring of a large, complex, non-bank financial institution that poses a threat to the stability of our financial system.'[2]

Since the failure of Lehman Brothers regulators have been working, nationally and internationally, to establish new procedures. The global effort is taking place under the auspices of the Financial Stability Board. One approach would be for the authorities to finance the wind-down of trading positions themselves. Another would be to empower them to oblige creditors to take a forced 'haircut' – in other words to accept a lower than par value for their assets. These solutions are complex to achieve nationally, and even harder when there is a cross-border dimension, as Paul Tucker of the Bank of England (who leads this international work) points out.[3] His conclusion: that 'a lot rests on whether we can resolve distressed LCFIs. We need to answer the big questions', must be correct. But there are no clear answers yet.

Other potential remedies to the too big to fail problem are

more controversial. The Volcker rule is one example (Section 15). There are also those who would argue for a more radical approach and for limiting the implicit state guarantee to narrow banks performing a tight range of functions which are essential for retail depositors and the financial system.[4] The IMF and others have argued for graduated capital require-ments, and a levy on bank balance sheets above a certain size, which would reflect the existence of implicit state support. Such a levy would, in economic terms, be a kind of insurance premium paid to the government for the potential availability of support.

Critics of these measures, while accepting the theory of the incentive argument, are sceptical of whether it is possible to define a subset of systemic institutions and treat them dif-ferently. They note that some smaller banks, like Northern Rock, were rescued too, although they would not have been regarded as systemic institutions beforehand. The issue of 'too big to fail' is partly one of political appetite for failure, therefore. The crisis also showed that some firms (Lehman being one) were 'too connected to fail' rather than simply too large.[5] How is it possible to cope with that problem simply by taxing size? Bankers also argue that some institutions are very big because they perform valuable economic services to very big clients, whom they could not effectively serve were they smaller. That case is very hard to prove one way or another. Haldane of the Bank of England is very sceptical.

And all the potential remedies for 'too big to fail' may fall at the credibility fence. In other words, whatever governments say in advance about institutions they will or will not rescue, firms and investors will be influenced by what they do, not what they say, and during the crisis many non-systemic firms were effectively underwritten by the authorities. So it will be hard to persuade investors that in future there will be some category of institution which will not be so rescued. On this argument, the fundamental response to the problem lies with higher capital in the banking system overall, to reduce the risk of failure to a lower level.

There is one further dimension of the problem that is some-times described as the banks which are 'too big to rescue', in other words firms headquartered in countries whose authorities are too small to back the liabilities, both domestic and international, of their systems. Iceland was the extreme case of that problem. It was in practice unable to underwrite the losses of its own banks, and therefore imposed costs on taxpayers in the UK and the Netherlands. Ireland came close to being in that position and is shrinking its financial sector dramatically. It was even argued that the UK and Switzerland had financial sectors which were too large for their economies, although so far the market overall has not taken that view.

The outcome is likely to be that major international banks will in future be headquartered in locations where the financial credibility of the authorities is high. Where that is not the case, it will be difficult for banks to use branch structures to operate across borders. They may well be required by local regulators to set up separately capitalized subsidiaries, to ensure that there is financial backing held within the host jurisdiction. This trend will have some consequences in terms of the effective use of bank capital in the future. It may, overall, increase the cost of credit, but it is almost certainly an inevitable response to the Icelandic banking crisis in particular. In Europe, there is an alternative. The EU could set up a pan-European regulator with a central resolution authority. But the political will for such a move is lacking at present. The British government, under any party, will be firmly opposed.

References

1. The Pursuit of Financial Stability. Eddie George. Lecture at the London School of Economics. 1993. www.bankofengland.co.uk
2. Written Testimony of Tim Geithner. US House of Representatives' Financial Services Committee. 24 March 2009. www.house.gov
3. Resolution of Large and Complex Financial Institutions: The Big Issues. Paul Tucker. Remarks at the European Commission's Conference on Crisis Management. Brussels. 19 March 2010.
4. Narrow Banking: The Reform of Banking Regulation. John Kay. September 2009. www.johnkay.com
5. Rethinking the Financial Network. Andrew G. Haldane. Speech delivered at the Financial Student Association, Amsterdam. April 2009.

17

LIGHTING THE TOUCHPAPER – LIGHT TOUCH REGULATION

Criticism of so-called 'light touch' regulation and its contribution to the crisis is largely a UK phenomenon. The US regulatory system is far more intrusive, with far more regulatory bodies and individuals employed in them (Section 11). The phrase 'light touch regulation' is rarely heard on the western side of the Atlantic, while in the UK it was widely used by Ministers in the Labour governments of Tony Blair and Gordon Brown, often to distinguish the UK approach from that taken in the US, and linked with thinly disguised attempts to attract mobile international financial business to London.

Ed Balls, while the Treasury Minister responsible for the City, noted that London's success in recent years had been built, among other things, on 'light touch, principles-based regulation'.[1] Gordon Brown referred to 'not just a light touch, but a limited touch'.[2]

The praise of light touch regulation was not exclusive to Labour Ministers. Indeed, during the passing of the Financial Services and Markets Act of 2001, which established the Financial Services Authority, Conservative spokesmen frequently warned against an over-intrusive approach by the new regulator. Vince Cable for the Liberal Democrats argued that financial regulation should be 'done on a light touch basis' in June 1999.[3] Subsequently, the political rhetoric has changed completely, with Ed Balls saying the advocates of light touch regulation (including himself, presumably) have been 'routed',[4] and opposition politicians competing to sound tougher than Ministers.

There is no clear definition of what is meant by 'light touch regulation'. Regulators themselves have almost never used the phrase, except to criticize it, talking instead about risk-based or principles-based regulation. Risk-based regulation is typically defined as an attempt 'to focus regulatory effort at the place of maximum effect in avoiding the worst outcomes for the greatest numbers and allocate resources accordingly'.[5] Principles-based regulation 'takes a high level approach to making rules and has the virtue of brevity . . . principles-based regulation is difficult to circumvent, but exceptions usually need to be allowed for, and if exceptions are unclear or are left unstated, the principles themselves can be hard to interpret and apply, leading to uncertainty.' The FSA has argued that principles-based regulation is not a 'light touch' approach, in that it can allow the regulator to enforce against firms based on general principles of acceptable behaviour in relation to customers. For example, even if the rulebook had not envisaged the specific practice involved, if it did not 'treat customers fairly' the firm could nonetheless be fined or otherwise disciplined. Financial firms have often argued against principles-based regulation on the grounds that it made them vulnerable to imprecise charges.

There are other possible definitions. One, which has been advanced by senior regulators in the United States, especially at the SEC, as a criticism of the UK, is that light touch regulation involves less enforcement. It is true that fewer enforcement actions are typically brought by the FSA than the SEC. UK regulators would argue, however, that lower enforcement effort is not necessarily associated with more abusive practices, in that it can be as effective to use informal measures to cause firms to change their behaviour. Also, in relation to the financial crisis specifically, it is not clear that market practices in securities markets were a decisive influence.

Another possible definition is that there are simply smaller numbers of regulators in the UK, in relation to the size of the financial sector, than there are elsewhere, and particularly in the United States. The FSA, which regulates the whole financial sector in the United Kingdom, employs fewer than 4,000 people, even after its recent expansion, while there are many multiples of that number in all the different regulatory bodies in the United States. The UK regime also places more reliance on the work of external auditors, and does not typically employ on-site regulators located within firms, as is usually the case in the United States. These differences in regulatory philosophy are marked, but it is not clear that there is any robust relationship between a scale of regulatory effort and success in promoting financial stability. The value-added of large teams of on-site examiners, examining the details of individual loans, is hard to discern.

Finally, it is argued that the FSA's approach to regulatory capital was in some ways weaker than that pursued elsewhere, even though the main standards being applied were global in their reach. There is some evidence that the FSA was more ready than some other regulators to accept various forms of hybrid capital instrument, which proved less robust than anticipated during the financial crisis. It is fair to say, though, that that feature of 'light touch' regulation was never advanced as a competitive distinguishing feature of the UK regime to attract banks. In any event it applied largely to British domestic-oriented institutions. Few foreign-owned banks are headquartered in London, and therefore subject to capital requirements set by the FSA.

Some commentators say that light touch regulation was in fact always a myth. *Daily Telegraph* editor Jeremy Warner maintained that 'in fact there was never any such thing as light touch regulation. The establishment of the FSA led to an unprecedented flood of rules and regulations.'[6] Indeed, Prime Minister Tony Blair, in May 2005,[7] attacked the FSA's intrusiveness, arguing that its activities were 'hugely inhibiting of efficient business by perfectly respectable companies that have never defrauded anyone'. On that occasion, the FSA Chairman found himself defending the authority's proportionate approach, a reversal of the normal roles.

But the crisis did bring about some rethinking of the UK regime. The Turner review published in March 2009[8] included some retrospective criticisms of the UK regime. Turner argued that in future there would need to be more and higher quality capital, recognizing that new capital rules needed to be agreed on a global basis. He argued that regulators in future would need to take a closer interest in the risk management of individual firms, no longer trusting those firms to manage risks themselves. They would need to be prepared to challenge the strategies of financial institutions more robustly, and indeed to adopt a more intrusive approach to approving the appointments of key individuals in senior positions. Taken together, those changes will amount to a significant tightening of regulation. It remains to be seen whether they will be more effective in promoting financial stability in the future.

References

1. Speech by Ed Balls, Economic Secretary to the Treasury, at the Tokyo Stock Exchange. 6 November 2006. www.hm-treasury.gov
2. Speech by Gordon Brown to the CBI Interactive Conference. 26 November 2005. www.cbi.org
3. Quoted in Vincent Cable: Beneath the Halo. Mehdi Hasan. September 2009. www.newstatesman.com
4. Ed Balls at the Labour Party Conference 2008, quoted in *The Independent*. 23 September 2008. www.independent.co.uk
5. Themes and Trends in Regulatory Reform. Regulatory Reform Committee. House of Commons. July 2009. www.publications.parliament.uk
6. The City Doesn't Need Any More Rules. Jeremy Warner. 6 July 2009. www.telegraph.co.uk
7. Speech on Compensation Culture. Tony Blair. 26 May 2005. Institute of Public Policy Research. www.ippr.org.uk
8. The Turner Review: A Regulatory Response to the Global Banking Crisis. Financial Services Authority. March 2009. www.fsa.gov.uk

18

THERE WERE THREE PEOPLE IN THE MARRIAGE – UK REGULATION

In September 2007, the UK experienced its first bank run, complete with queues of depositors outside branches, for well over a century. Northern Rock was an aggressive mortgage lender – a former building society which had converted to banking status. It had grown its market share rapidly and, at times, was originating almost a quarter of all mortgages in the UK. Its funding depended on a particular securitization model, which meant that it was one of the first institutions to struggle to secure liquidity when the securitization market dried up in the midsummer of 2007. By September it was clear that it could no longer finance its mortgage book in the market.

The authorities explored a range of options, including a takeover by Lloyds Bank: see *Banking on the Future* by Davies and Green for an extended discussion of the events of that period.[1] But the Lloyds takeover option failed when the Bank of England declined to provide a liquidity guarantee, and all other options to find private sector purchasers (even Richard Branson was considered) petered out during the autumn. Eventually, therefore, the bank was nationalized – a very unappealing option for a Labour government whose leadership had come to power with a well-publicized renunciation of the party's previous commitment to nationalizing the commanding heights of the economy.

The handling of this episode looked very clumsy, and

damaged confidence in the UK financial system. There were many well-sourced reports of fundamental differences between the Treasury, the Bank of England, and the Financial Services Authority. This episode therefore focused public attention on the Tripartite Agreement between the three authorities, which, for a time, was identified as a major cause of the crisis in the United Kingdom.

When the Labour government created the Financial Services Authority in 1997 a Memorandum of Understanding was drawn up with the Bank of England and the Treasury[2] which was intended to govern the relationships between the three. In principle, the Treasury was responsible for the institutional structure of the regulatory system and for the legislation behind it, the Bank of England was described as 'contributing to the maintenance of the stability of the financial system as a whole', while the FSA was given the responsibility of authorizing and supervising individual banks and other financial institutions under the Financial Services and Markets Act 2000 (the author was one of those responsible for the MoU at the time). In 1997, internal controversy centred on the extent to which the Bank of England could be allowed discretion to perform support operations without reference back to the Treasury. The first version (it was revised in 2006) provided that the Treasury could prevent the Bank of England from extending liquidity support, but not that it could require it so to do. That drafting reflected the ancestry of the relationship between the Treasury and the Bank. The Treasury suspected the Bank of England of having extended support to institutions (such as Johnson Matthey) which were not systemic, in order to preserve banks with which it had a close relationship, or indeed to cover up failings in its supervision.

The MoU attracted relatively little attention at the time. But when it was suspected during the 2007 crisis that the three different authorities were taking different views, attention began to focus on its terms and, particularly, on who had the final responsibility for making decisions in relation to the support of individual institutions, and to the liquidity support of the system as a whole.

The Treasury Select Committee of Parliament carried out an inquiry. Their report 'The Run On The Rock' was very critical.[3]

In the evidence sessions, Willem Buiter argued that 'the notion that the institution that has the knowledge of the individual banks that may or may not be in trouble would be a different institution from the one that has the money, the resources, to act upon the observation that a particular bank needs lender of last resort support is risky . . . it is an invitation to disaster, to delay, and to wrong decisions.'[4] The authorities, somewhat uncomfortably, defended the system and were unwilling to expose the differences of view which had impeded the handling of the Northern Rock problem. The report's eventual conclusion was that the run on Northern Rock 'represents a significant failure of the Tripartite system' but did not conclude in favour of wholesale change: 'instead, we want to see it reformed, with clear leadership and stronger powers'. The committee was implicitly critical of the Treasury's lack of effective authority over the other two institutions. They also believed that the Bank of England had become too distant from the financial markets following the 1997 reform and made a number of recommendations to strengthen the financial stability wing of the Bank.

In a subsequent report on banking supervision in the UK, the House of Lords Economic Affairs Committee went further.[5] They argued that the Bank of England needed institution-specific information and a closer understanding of the daily operations of the financial markets to function effectively during a crisis and recommended that the government should ensure that it had such information. They proposed that the government should 'allocate responsibility for macro prudential supervision to the Bank of England', recognizing that there would be some overlap with the FSA's responsibilities.

The government eventually accepted that there was a case for change, but rejected a major structural overhaul, in favour of setting up a new Council for Financial Stability which would include the three authorities. 'It will not only deal with immediate issues, but will monitor system-wide financial stability and respond to long-term risks as they emerge.' The council would be set up on a formal statutory basis, unlike the MoU, which had no legal underpinning.[6]

The Conservatives, however, did not accept the conclusion that the Tripartite system was fundamentally sound.

They commissioned a review from James Sassoon, a former Treasury official and previously an adviser to Gordon Brown, which analysed the problem in some depth. It recommended that the Bank should conduct 'a continuous high level dialogue with market participants' and supported the location of macro-prudential responsibility there. It also canvassed a number of options for reform, without recommending any particular option, though broadly agreeing that the FSA should remain responsible for handling the problems of individual institutions.[7]

But by July of 2009 the Conservative Party's view had hardened. In a White Paper called 'From Crisis to Confidence: Plan for Sound Banking'[8] they were far more outspoken in their criticism of the regulatory regime. They described the Tripartite framework as 'confused and fragmented . . . the result is that nobody identified the underlying problems as they built up and nobody had the power or authority to act once the crisis hit. We need fundamental reform.' The reform they recommended went well beyond the options canvassed by Sassoon and proposed making the Bank of England responsible for prudential regulation, both macro and micro, of all 'significant institutions, including insurance companies'. (The paper also committed a future Conservative government to 'fight any new attempt to create an executive pan-European supervisor'.) These conclusions seemed informed as much by political considerations as by an analysis of the underlying problems. The Conservative Party had settled on a pre-election narrative which placed primary responsibility for the financial crisis in the UK on Gordon Brown, and specifically linked that to the regulatory reform he introduced in 1997. The proposals caused some surprise in financial circles, and were not widely supported. A *Financial Times* survey reported that they 'drew particular scorn' among bankers.[9]

How significant were the failings of the Tripartite system? And how far can it be said that a flawed regulatory structure was a decisive factor in creating the crisis, or damaging the authorities' ability to handle it when it arrived?

Most will acknowledge that the Northern Rock affair itself was badly handled. But the most powerful criticism made by the Treasury Select Committee was of the absence of leadership, which was primarily a Treasury problem. When the MoU was drafted it was clear that the Treasury, which appoints the heads of the other two agencies, had the ultimate responsibility for decision making. In fact the Tripartite committee did not meet once between 1997 and 2003 at the level of the principals, which included Gordon Brown as Chancellor of the Exchequer. But at deputy level it met frequently and developed habits of cooperation. Those habits did not appear to have carried through, unfortunately, to the circumstances in which the principals became closely involved in 2007, by which time there was new personnel at the Treasury, the Bank of England and the FSA.

Was this breakdown attributable to the structure itself? The answer is unclear. When it is necessary to consider support for a particular institution, or indeed for a number of financial firms, it is inevitable that finance ministries are brought into the picture. While the central bank is able to assist with liquidity, if there is an issue of solvency – as evidently there was in the case of Northern Rock – then the finance ministry must agree. In some countries, the central bank is also the banking supervisor, as was the case in the UK before 1997, but in at least fifty countries the central bank does not carry responsibility for institutional supervision. So in all those places, some version of a Tripartite arrangement is in operation. Indeed there are many who believe that the clarity of the UK's Memorandum of Understanding in 1997 was a model for others. And the post-crisis reforms, both globally and in the European Union, envisaged bodies which group together regulators, central banks and finance ministries.

More broadly, it is difficult to identify any clear relationship between the regulatory structure in operation in individual countries and 'success' or 'failure' in handling the financial crisis. It is sometimes argued that Spain did relatively well, with the Bank of Spain introducing innovative arrangements for dynamic provisioning which strengthened the balance sheets of their major banks. But two other countries which managed conspicuously well through the crisis are Australia and Canada. They operate regulatory structures which do not involve the central bank in institutional supervision, and which indeed are similar to those in the United Kingdom post

1997. The model which comes closest to the proposition put forward by the Conservative Party in July 2009 is in operation in the Netherlands, where the central bank has prudential supervision for all financial firms (though it is not also the monetary authority). Arguably, the Dutch financial system was more seriously impaired than any other in Europe except perhaps those of Iceland and Ireland. Had a consortium led by the Royal Bank of Scotland not bought ABN Amro just before the crisis erupted, almost the whole of the Dutch banking system would have been on life support from the State.

So the clearest lesson from the crisis is that there is a need for close and effective coordination between regulators, central bankers and finance ministries. There must be suitable institutional arrangements and habits of cooperation to ensure that rapid decisions can be made in a timely manner. But the crisis did not provide any decisive evidence in favour of any particular institutional model of supervision, or any particular role for the central bank. The arguments of principle about the central bank role in supervision and in financial stability are set out in more detail in Davies and Green.[10] They point to a need for closer involvement in financial markets than the Bank of England maintained in the years before the crisis, but not necessarily to a case for structural reform in the UK.

References

1. *Banking on the Future: The Fall and Rise of Central Banking.* Howard Davies and David Green. Princeton University Press. 2010.
2. Memorandum of Understanding between the Bank of England, Financial Services Authority and HM Treasury. 22 March 2006. www.fsa.gov.uk
3. The Run on the Rock. Report by the Treasury Committee. House of Commons. 24 January 2008. www.publications.parliament.uk/
4. Oral Evidence Ev329. Willem Buiter – in the above report.
5. Banking Supervision and Regulation Report. Economic Affairs Committee. House of Lords. 19 May 2009. www.publications. parliament.uk/
6. Reforming Financial Markets. Statement of Alistair Darling at the House of Commons. 8 July 2009. www.hm-treasury.gov.uk

7. Tripartite Review – A Review to the Shadow Chancellor. James Sassoon. March 2009. www.conservatives.com

8. From Crisis to Confidence: Plan for Sound Banking. George Osborne. Policy White Paper. July 2009. www.conservatives.com

9. Osborne Fails to Convince City. Patrick Jenkins and Megan Murphy. *The Financial Times.* 28 April 2010. www.ft.com

10. *Global Financial Regulation: The Essential Guide.* Howard Davies and David Green. Polity Press. Cambridge. 2008.

19

A FAILURE OF
COORDINATION

The financial crisis of 2007 onwards has been described as the first crisis of globalization. Although different countries and different financial systems were affected in different ways, almost no country or financial institution was spared entirely. The degree of contagion from one financial market to another was remarkable. Disturbances in the subprime mortgage market in the United States triggered a collapse in equity prices in Shanghai. Some of these linkages came as a surprise to governments and regulators, who did not seem as well integrated as the markets themselves. So attention was focused on the global network of financial regulators. How did this network function? Should it not have been able to identify emerging risks and act to head them off?

The global network of regulators is extremely complex. There are distinct groupings for banking, securities and insurance, each with regional sub-groups. Accountants and auditors are overseen separately. Central banks maintain their own network, based in Basel, and the International Financial Institutions all have partial roles. The FSA, the UK's single regulator, was a member of over 150 bodies or standing committees.

In *Global Financial Regulation: The Essential Guide* by Davies and Green, published in early 2008, the authors say that 'the international regulatory system has developed in a piecemeal fashion. It has been reasonably successful in maintaining financial stability in a fast changing world, but it is now seriously out of date and may not be adequate to address the challenges such change will bring. The global committees, whose structure is rooted in an old-fashioned breakdown of financial activity into the "sectors" of banking, insurance and securities, need radical reform if they are to keep pace with the rapid evolution of financial markets. The market turmoil of the summer of 2007, originating in the US subprime mortgage market, demonstrated vividly that the technology of credit transfer had developed to the point where it is hard to determine where risks now lie – and it is quite impossible for the regulator of a single sector to do so.'[1]

The authors argued for a strengthening of the Financial Stability Forum which had been put in place after the Asian financial crisis of the late 1990s. The Forum did group all the key regulatory bodies and committees in one place, but, as its name implied, had no authority over them and undertook little independent work of its own.

These criticisms of the global system were not new. In 1987, Gerald Corrigan, then President of the New York Federal Reserve Bank, said, 'the pace of change and innovation in financial markets and institutions here and around the world has increased enormously, as has the speed, volume and value of financial transactions. The period has also seen a greatly heightened degree of aggressive competition in the financial sector. All of this has taken place in the context of a legal and a regulatory framework which is increasingly outdated and ill-equipped to meet the challenges of the day.'[2] Little progress in resolving these problems was made in the twenty years following that diagnosis.

The G20 Summits of 2008–2009 broadly accepted that the system needed strengthening at global level. In April 2009, G20 leaders agreed in London that the Financial Stability Forum be renamed the Financial Stability Board, with a broadened mandate to promote financial stability, expanded membership, stronger institutional basis, and enhanced capacity.[3] They did not, however, endow it with any new formal authority to direct the other regulatory groupings. In practice, G20 Ministers do now increasingly look to the FSB for coordination, but the difficulty of agreeing any cession of national powers to a global body is marked. Although, in the area of merchandise trade, there is a World Trade Organization, with some enforcement authority over individual states, there is no equivalent supranational body in the financial sector and currently no plan to create one. Governments have been reluctant to contemplate such a step, even within the European Union, where arguably the need for a pan-European regulatory body is more marked.

As the crisis developed, understanding of its unusual characteristics and, particularly, of the network implications has grown. Andy Haldane of the Bank of England has argued that it has become both more complex and more homogenous at the same time.[4] 'Securitization increased the dimensionality, and thus complexity of the financial network. Nodes grew in size and interconnections between them multiplied . . . The financial cat's cradle became dense and opaque. As a result, the precise source and location of underlying claims became anyone's guess . . . diversification strategies by individual firms generated heightened uncertainty across the system as a whole.' On Haldane's analysis, 'the scale and interconnectivity of the international financial network has increased significantly over the past two decades. Nodes have ballooned, increasing roughly 14-fold. And links have become both fatter and more frequent, increasing roughly 6-fold. The network has become remarkably more dense and complex.'

The consequence is a financial system with greater interconnectivity and more vulnerability to shocks. Haldane's proposed response involves enhanced mapping of these interconnections, more global regulation of them to enhance the 'restricted visibility' of risk transfers and, perhaps, more robust central mechanisms.

The existing networks of regulators, built, as they are, on the principle of achieving consensus, with rules implemented country by country on a 'best endeavours' basis, and with no effective enforcement mechanism, are not well structured to respond to that challenge. As a result, there are continued calls for further enhancements in regulatory cooperation, and even for the creation of a central body with global regulatory powers, though the precise nature of the powers that would be needed to enhance both oversight and regulation of this complex set of networks has not yet been articulated.

References

1. *Global Financial Regulation: The Essential Guide*. Howard Davies and David Green. Polity Press. Cambridge. 2008.
2. Financial Market Structure: A Longer View. Gerald Corrigan. Federal Reserve Bank of New York. 1987.
3. Declaration on Strengthening the Financial System – Annex to London Summit Communiqué. G20 Summit. 2 April 2009. www.g20.org
4. Rethinking the Financial Network. Andrew G. Haldane. Speech delivered at the Financial Student Association, Amsterdam. April 2009.

20

PARADISE LOST
OFFSHORE CENTRES

The French phrase 'paradis fiscaux' is far more evocative than 'offshore centres', its English equivalent. The difference in terminology also reflects different attitudes. Finance Ministers in Anglo-Saxon countries may not be enthusiastic about the implications of offshore centres for their tax revenues from wealthy citizens, but they tend to tolerate offshore jurisdictions as an unavoidable, if tiresome feature of the global scene. Many of the largest centres are, of course, former British territories or offshore dependencies.

Some of them, like the Cayman Islands or Bermuda, play significant roles in the international financial markets: the first as a prime location for hedge funds, the second as a reinsurance centre. The attractions of offshore centres are threefold: taxation (where the rates and coverage of tax are often significantly lower), transparency (bank secrecy is much more common), and in some cases less intrusive regulation. The first point, differential tax regimes, is not easy for other countries to address, except indirectly through controls on what their own citizens do in those jurisdictions. The second issue has been addressed in various ways, notably through money laundering controls imposed by the OECD's Financial Action Task Force. But it remains easier to hide financial assets and financial transactions in the offshore world than it is elsewhere.

The third question, the possibility of weaker and 'more flexible' regulation, is more complex. Several attempts have been made to persuade or oblige offshore centres to follow international regulatory standards. A comprehensive attempt to classify them into the good, the bad and the ugly was made by the Financial Stability Forum in 1999. This had some effect and the largest centres claim, with some validity, that they broadly meet the main requirements of the international regulatory codes. Financial sector assessments carried out by the IMF have tended to confirm that.

But when the crisis erupted it was not long before those who were naturally predisposed to identify offshore centres as a problem began to argue that they were at the heart of the crisis. This argument was advanced particularly by French politicians in the run-up to the Pittsburgh and London Summits. Nicolas Sarkozy said, 'we must ask some difficult questions, such as about offshore centres' and his Prime Minister, François Fillon, described them as 'black holes'. In his view they ought not to exist and 'their disappearance must be part of the reconstruction of the international financial system'.[1] The French were not alone. Vince Cable, the Liberal Democrat finance spokesman in the UK, linked them to the growth of the shadow banking sector and off-balance sheet vehicles: 'much of the shadow banking sector, a major contributor to the economic crisis, was also only possible because of tax haven secrecy'.[2] These political pressures, and a lively NGO campaign led by organizations like the Secours Catholique[3] and Transparency International,[4] led to the G20 including a statement on offshore centres in their communication following the London Summit. The leaders committed themselves to 'take action against non-cooperative jurisdictions, including tax havens. We stand ready to deploy sanctions to protect our public finances and financial systems. The era of banking secrecy is over.'[5] The G20 also identified a link between tax havens and the financial crisis, in stating, 'removing practices that facilitate tax evasion is part of a broader drive to clean up one of the more controversial sides of a globalized economy'.[6]

These statements left unclear the role which offshore centres were supposed to have played. While tax avoidance undoubtedly has adverse consequences for the fiscal positions of many countries, and fiscal problems became more and more significant as the crisis evolved, it did not seem to be closely linked to the run-up to the crisis. The regulatory argument, however, was not clearly spelled out.

Those who have addressed the question directly have not identified a strong link. So Avinash Persaud, a member of a UN committee on international finance, said, 'offshore centres have nothing to do with the crisis, they tend to be small states so they are very easy targets. But this is a red herring.'[7] Adair Turner in his report in March 2009 noted, 'it is important to recognize that the role of offshore banking centres was not central in the origins of the current crisis. Some securitized investment vehicles were registered in offshore locations; but regulation of banks could have required these to be brought on balance sheet and captured within the ambit of group capital adequacy requirements. And many of the problems arose from the inadequate regulation of the trading activities of banks operating through onshore legal entities in major financial centres such as London or New York.'[8]

Loomer and Mafini, of the Oxford University Centre for Business and Taxation, broadly agree, and conclude that the shadow banking system was poorly regulated not only offshore but also in the main onshore centres, although they do note that 'the location of off-balance sheet and off-budget vehicles in certain jurisdictions certainly does not contribute to the transparency of the system'.[9]

As the crisis rolled on, the focus on offshore centres became somewhat diluted. The British government commissioned a review by a former regulator designed to prod those centres to meet international standards on tax transparency and financial regulation, and to do more to tackle financial crime, notably money laundering.[10] But there seemed to be little global political appetite for a more fundamental assault on the independence and privileges of offshore centres. If they are black holes, as the French assert, then they are likely to remain at least dark grey, even after the post-crisis reforms.

References

1. Crise Financière et Paradis Fiscaux. Transparence International (France). 24 October 2008. http://diploweb.com
2. The Offensive Secrecy of Tax Havens. Vincent Cable. *The Guardian*. 23 September 2009. www.guardian.co.uk
3. Les Paradis Fiscaux sont au Coeur de la Crise. Interview with Michel Roy by Nicolas Gateau. Pélerin. 18 November 2008. www.pelerin. info
4. Les Paradis Fiscaux, Agents de la Crise Financière. Attac France. 11 February 2009. www.france.attac.org
5. London Summit Communiqué. G20 Summit. 2 April 2009. www. g20.org
6. Ibid.
7. Offshore Blame seen as Crisis Red Herring. Lisa Jucca. Reuters. 19 March 2010. http://us.mobile.reuters.com
8. The Turner Review: A Regulatory Response to the Global Banking Crisis. Financial Services Authority. March 2009. www.fsa.gov.uk
9. Tax Havens and the Financial Crisis. Geoffrey Loomer and Giorgia Maffini. Oxford University Centre for Business Taxation. April 2009.
10. British Offshore Financial Centres: Final Report. HM Treasury. 29 October 2009. www.hm-treasury.gov.uk

D ACCOUNTANTS, AUDITORS AND RATING AGENCIES

The activities of the quasi-regulators in the private sector have also come under the spotlight.

The operation of fair value accounting, whose rules obliged firms to mark down their securitization assets to market prices, was argued to have contributed to a downward spiral of value destruction (Section 21). More generally, auditors did not raise the alarm, even in respect of firms in danger of imminent collapse (22).

Ratings agencies have found themselves under intense scrutiny. They had granted high ratings to securitizations which lost all, or almost all, their value. Did that not reveal a fundamental flaw in their operating model, and in their regulation (23)?

21

SHOOT THE MESSENGER
FAIR VALUE
ACCOUNTING

Setting accounting standards has been a surprisingly controversial activity in recent years. Since well before the crisis, there
have been serious tensions within the standard-setting groups
themselves, between standard setters and politicians, between
accountants and prudential regulators, and between prudential and securities regulators. There has also been transatlantic
tension. The International Accounting Standards Board (IASB)
has for many years been working on a set of International
Financial Reporting Standards (IFRS) designed to promote
convergence between American standards, US GAAP, set by
the Financial Accounting Standards Board (FASB), and those
used elsewhere.

The process of convergence has exposed fault-lines between
the US and continental Europe. European politicians have
often believed that the American authorities were not acting
in good faith in declaring their 'in principle' support for one
set of international accounting standards, noting that the
SEC had never fully committed to replacing US GAAP. By
contrast, the US authorities were suspicious of political interference in the affairs of the FASB, both through the European
Commission and directly from European governments. In
a joint article, President Sarkozy of France and Chancellor
Merkel of Germany wrote, 'we will not allow capital requirements and accounting standards unjustifiably to reduce the

lending capacity of European banks . . . so we are calling for amendments to the accounting rules which are so important for our economies' recovery.'[1] In his opening speech at the World Economic Forum in Davos in 2010, Sarkozy ridiculed aspects of US accounting standards: 'we got to the point, ladies and gentlemen, of valuing a firm's asset at the market price, forgetting that the market constantly fluctuates'.[2] As Andy Haldane of the Bank of England has commented, 'Among Heads of State in some of the biggest countries in the world, accounting standards for derivatives have generated levels of fear and consternation usually reserved for non-financial weapons of mass destruction.'[3]

American standard setters resent these political interventions. Robert Hertz, the Chairman of the FASB, called on the IASB to resist political pressure. 'The US wants to make sure that the standards it uses come out of a standard setter which has the appropriate public policy objectives, and is not being geared or harassed to do things in a way that is not consistent with that public policy objective . . . as one Congressman once said to me; it will be a cold day in hell when I let a Frenchman tell me what to do.'[4]

A second tension was between those who favoured fair value accounting, often known as mark to market accounting, and those who argued that banks held many loans with the expectation of holding them to maturity, and that a fair value approach was not appropriate. Investment banks typically took the former view, recognizing that almost any asset on their balance sheet was effectively 'held for sale'. European commercial banks argued that it was nonsense for them to be obliged to write down a loan as soon as they made it, as a rigorous fair value approach would require. They maintained that it presumed the existence of deep and liquid markets, which was by no means always the case. Nonetheless, in the years leading up to the crisis, the advocates of fair value accounting were in the ascendancy, on both sides of the Atlantic.

A third tension was between accounting standard setters and prudential regulators. As Adair Turner put it in 2010, 'among bank prudential regulators and central banks, there is a belief that existing bank accounting standards were among the factors contributing to the crisis, inducing procyclicality and credit provision and pricing. And there is a demand that bank accounting standards must reflect the concerns of prudential regulators. There is a belief that banks are different, and that accounting standards need to recognize this. Among many securities analysts and investors, however, and among some accounting standard setters, there is a belief that accounts are for investors and not for regulators, that they must tell the truth as it exists at one particular point in time, and that any influence of prudential regulators on bank accounting standards could be a Trojan horse for a wider politicization.'[5]

He acknowledged that the tension was also present within the regulatory community, between the pure securities regulators and others with prudential responsibilities. He further suggested that there were tensions between the IASB, which 'has been sympathetic to the idea that it must be involved in close dialogue with prudential regulators', and the FASB, which 'has been more wedded to the "accounts are for investors" only philosophy, and the philosophy that banks, in their accounting, should be treated no differently from anybody else'.

These underlying tensions came together in the financial crisis, especially when subprime securitizations began to fall in value precipitously. Accounting standards required banks to mark these securitizations to market prices, at a time when those prices were influenced by a crisis of liquidity. Many bankers complained bitterly. William Isaac, a former FDIC Chairman, argued that 'the accounting system is destroying too much capital, and therefore diminishing bank lending capacity by some $5 trillion. It's due to the accounting system, and I can't come up with any other explanation.'[6] Banks were being forced to mark their illiquid assets down to unrealistic fire sale prices. The fair value rules 'have destroyed hundreds of billions of dollars of capital in our financial system . . . I'm asking for a very bad rule to be suspended until we can think about this more . . . it is my fervent hope that the SEC will recommend that we abandon mark to market accounting altogether.' Martin Sullivan, when Chief Executive of AIG, made a similar point.[7] Credit Suisse argued that 'the stock of leveraged credit assets overhanging the market now, combined with the acceleration of margin calls, forced liquidations and capital write-downs, creates a self-reinforcing dynamic towards even greater capital destruction at the banks'.[8]

How far can fair value accounting be blamed for the market crash?

The controversy on valuation accounting goes back over a century, but the particular statement of financial accounting standards on fair value measurements, which was in operation as the crisis began, dates from a standard issued in September 2006 by the FASB in the US (FAS 157). In Europe, there was a parallel standard for the accounting of financial assets (IAS 39), which was not identical, but which had similar consequences. The rule suggested that loans and debt securities that are held for investment or to maturity should be carried at advertised cost, unless they are deemed to be impaired, but if they are available for sale or held for sale, they are required to be carried at fair value or the lower of cost or fair value. The rule requires a mark to market price, though in some cases, where appropriate market prices were not available, the standard allows what is known as 'mark to model', in other words the use of prices derived from calculations related to the underlying assets. This approach was described by Warren Buffet as 'mark to myth'.[9]

The logic seems powerful, but it was tested to destruction in the unusual market circumstances of 2008. A somewhat more sophisticated criticism of the problem came from the Institute of International Finance.[10] In a memorandum, they argued that 'often dramatic write downs of sound assets required under the current implementation of fair value accounting adversely affect market sentiment, in turn leading to further write downs, margin calls and capital impacts in a downwards spiral that may lead to large-scale fire sales of assets, and destabilizing procyclical feedback effects. These damaging feedback effects worsen liquidity problems and contribute to the conversion of liquidity problems into solvency problems.'

These criticisms were heard in Congress. As the crisis evolved, political interest in accounting standards was not exclusively a European preserve. Under the Emergency Economic Stabilization Act of 2008, the SEC was given the authority to suspend the application of FAS 157 if it determined that to do so would be in the public interest. The Act also required the SEC to conduct a study on mark to market accounting standards, which it published in December of that year, and which led it to decide not to suspend mark to market accounting. The accounting standard setters internationally remained unrepentant. David Tweedie, the Chair of the IASB, said, 'my personal view is that showing the changes in values of these [illiquid, structured credit] securities, even if imperfect, provides much needed transparency and enables markets to adjust in a necessary and even painful manner'.[11] The Chief Executive of the Institute of Chartered Accountants of England and Wales, Michael Izza, told the British Parliament, 'painful though fair value may be, it has got the news out much faster than other methodologies might have done, leading to speedier actions to deal with the situation. It is very important that we do not seek to shoot the messenger.'[12]

In Brussels, Nicolas Veron of the Breugel Institute asserted that 'fair value accounting is the wrong scapegoat for this crisis'.[13] He argued that the notion that current standards should be suspended or amended 'disregards the negative impact which would result from the loss of data presently supplied by financial reporting and compliance with the standards. And it unhelpfully muddies the distinction between accounting and prudential concerns, which correspond to different objects and should be more carefully distinguished.' Recognizing some of the criticisms as valid, he noted nonetheless that 'fair value accounting as currently prescribed by IFRS and US GAAP can be described in an analogy with Churchill's portrayal of democracy, as the worst system with the exception of all others'. The UK Treasury Select Committee said they 'did not consider fair value accounting to be a suitable scapegoat for the hubris, poor risk controls and bad decisions of the banking sector'.[14]

In a study for the Frankfurt-based Centre for Financial Studies, Laux and Leuz concluded that 'while there may have been downward spirals or asset fire sales in certain markets, we find little evidence that these effects are the result of fair-value accounting'.[15]

But the SEC's review, and the IASB's reassertion of the fair value principle, did not end the argument. In a speech to the Council on Foreign Relations in Washington in March 2009,

Chairman Bernanke of the Federal Reserve said, 'we should review regulatory policies and accounting rules to ensure that they do not induce excessive procyclicality, that is, they do not overly magnify the ups and downs in the financial systems and in the economy'.[16] In April, the FASB did indeed ease the mark to market rules, giving more flexibility for institutions, especially when faced with valuing assets in inactive markets. The IASB produced an exposure draft on fair value measurement later in the year, in an attempt to reform IAS 39. The IASB said that their intention now was to define 'when fair value and cost-based accounting should be applied to financial instruments . . . extending the use of fair value has not been our motive or attempt in developing a new standard . . . the emphasis has been to define in a balanced and transparent way the appropriate criteria for classifying instruments to be measured at cost and at fair value . . . the IASB will not require that the loan book of banks be held at fair value.'[17]

This change of heart was seen as recognition that accounting standards needed to recognize the interests of prudential regulators. But some among those regulators remained concerned. Adair Turner argued in January 2010 that 'there is a strong case that the present accounting treatment contributes to the problem of procyclicality'.[18] This is so because the standard requires banks only to recognize known events which made their loans irrecoverable, and not to anticipate possible future events. 'As a result, this accounting treatment can attribute to a cycle of self-reinforcing responses which tends to exacerbate the volatility of credit extension and of the economic cycle, both on the way up and on the way down.' While recognizing that 'in the trading books in particular, there are many instruments for which there is no feasible alternative to a fair value approach, and noting that the criticisms of fair value in that area were heard only when the value of assets went down sharply, and not at a time when they rose rapidly, there are issues about what should be included in trading books for both regulatory and accounting periods'.

This pointed to the fundamental problem, which is that 'under the conditions of inherent uncertainty which govern financial contracts' there is no one true set of values. While mark to market accounting gives the value at which one firm, at a given moment in time, can liquidate its portfolio, if all firms try to liquidate a large proportion of their assets at the same time 'a transparent system of mark to market accounting with fluctuating and transparent prices may tend to induce the very collective behaviour which makes the measured mark to market values seem to be true'.[19] Turner argued, therefore, that there might need to be further changes to both accounting standards and to the approaches to loss recognition and to capital taken by prudential regulators. He thus reopened an old debate about the respective interests of regulators with a single-minded focus on protecting the interest of investors, and prudential regulators with a financial stability concern, both in respect to individual firms, and to the financial system as a whole. By contrast, Haldane of the Bank of England argues that 'with financial markets still thick with fog and filthy air, now would be an unfortunate time to starve balance sheets of the sunlight provided by fair values'.[20] Almost three years into the financial crisis, this fundamental problem of valuation is no nearer to resolution.

References

1. Pour une Europe qui protège. Nicolas Sarkozy and Angela Merkel. *Le Journal Du Dimanche*. 31 May 2009. English version available on www.ambafrance-uk.org
2. Opening Speech at the 40th World Economic Forum. Nicolas Sarkozy. Davos, 27 January 2010.
3. Fair Value in Foul Weather. Andrew Haldane. March 2010. http://bankofengland.co.uk/
4. Europe Must Stop its Meddling, says FASB Chief. Mario Christodoulou. *Accountancy Age*. 15 October 2009. www.accountancyage.com
5. Banks are Different: Should Accounting Reflect that Fact? Adair Turner. Speech at The Institute of Chartered Accountants in England and Wales. 21 January 2010.
6. Former FDIC Chief: Fair Value Caused the Crisis. David Katz. 29 October 2008. www.cfo.com
7. An Unforgiving Eye: Bankers Cry Foul over Fair Value Accounting Rules. Jennifer Hughes and Gillian Tett. *Financial Times*. 13 March 2008. www.ft.com
8. Ibid.

9. Berkshire Hathaway 2002 Annual Report. www.berkshire hathaway.com
10. Board of Directors' Discussion Memorandum on Valuation in Illiquid Markets. Institute of International Finance. 7 April 2008. www.iif.com
11. Remarks at the Empire Club of Canada. Sir David Tweedie. 25 April 2008.
12. Banking Crisis: Reforming Corporate Governance and Pay in the City. Report of the Treasury Committee, House of Commons. May 2009. www.publications.parliament.uk/
13. Fair Value Accounting Is the Wrong Scapegoat for This Crisis. Nicolas Véron. Bruegel Policy Contribution. May 2008. www.bruegel.org/
14. Banking Crisis, Treasury Committee Report.
15. Did Fair-Value Accounting Contribute to the Financial Crisis? Christian Laux and Christian Leuz. CFS Working Paper No. 2009/22. October 2009. www.ifk-cfs.de
16. A Conversation with Ben Bernanke. Conference at the Council on Foreign Relations. 10 March 2009. www.cfr.org
17. Update to European Finance Ministers on Reforms to IAS 39 Financial Instruments. Sir David Tweedie. 20 October 2009. www. iasb.org
18. Banks are Different, Turner.
19. Ibid.
20. Fair Value in Foul Weather, Haldane.

22

TUNNEL VISION
THE AUDITORS

One striking feature of the crisis is that the firms which collapsed were given clean bills of health by their auditors shortly before they failed. Bear Stearns received an unqualified audit opinion on 28 January 2008, while by 14 March it had been forcibly taken over, with Federal Reserve assistance, by JP Morgan. Lehman Brothers received a clean opinion on its quarterly accounts on 10 July and filed for bankruptcy on 14 September 2008. Should auditors not have raised the alarm earlier? Were auditors another set of watchdogs which lay peacefully sleeping while the crisis erupted around them?

In 'Financial Crisis and the Silence of the Auditors', Prem Sikka, of the Centre for Global Accountability at the University of Essex, has set out the accusations. He notes that the key text on UK corporate governance states that 'audits are a reassurance to all who have a financial interest in companies',[1] yet auditors acquiesced while banks showed assets at highly inflated values and used derivatives to inflate profits by hiding losses and hence risks. While there was information to suggest that some of the failed institutions were running dramatically high leverage ratios which threatened their survival, the auditors remained silent. 'How the auditors constructed audits to satisfy themselves that banks were a growing concern is open to conjecture, but the financial difficulties of many became publicly evident soon after receiving unqualified audit reports.' Sikka questions whether auditors are appropriately independent, given the additional non-auditing work they undertake for their clients. He suggests that 'the intensification of finance capitalism poses questions about the knowledge base of auditors'. Given the huge complexity of valuation problems related to complex derivatives, we may have 'reached the limits of conventional auditing technologies and ought to be considering alternative forms of accounting, disclosures and accountabilities'.

Investors have been critical, too. In a memorandum to the UK Treasury Select Committee, the Investment Management Association accused auditors of following accounting standards in 'an overly mechanistic way without applying sufficient professional judgement'.[2] They referred specifically to accounts where large liabilities held in off-balance sheet vehicles were not disclosed, where the agreements that linked the institutions to those off-balance sheet vehicles had not been properly interpreted and where the disclosures of valuation methodologies were inadequate, particularly where financial instruments were 'marked to model'. Furthermore, they argued that auditors should have raised more questions about the default risk of borrowers and the authentication procedures that have been followed.

The accounting profession has rejected these criticisms. In evidence to the UK Parliamentary Committee, Brendan Nelson, the Vice Chairman of KPMG, said, 'in the context of the statutory audit responsibilities for 2007, auditors, we believe, discharged their responsibilities professionally and with care and diligence'.[3] Furthermore, the audit inspection units of the Financial Reporting Council, the oversight body for the auditing profession in the UK, reported that the quality of auditing remained 'fundamentally sound with no systemic weaknesses'.[4] Professor Michael Power of the LSE added further independent support to the profession by agreeing that it was 'hard to conclude that financial auditing as a whole, or in specific cases, should be a major focus of blame for the financial crisis . . . external audit does not have a role at a price quite worth paying'.[5]

In its own report, the committee noted that it had received little evidence to suggest that the auditors failed to fulfil their duties as currently set out, 'but the fact that the audit process failed to highlight developing problems in the banking sector does cause us to question exactly how useful audit currently is. We are perturbed that the process results in "tunnel vision", where the big picture that shareholders want to see is lost in a sea of detail and regulatory disclosures.'[6]

In the United States, attention has focused on specific examples where auditors seem to have missed warning signs. So, for example, the insolvency examiner of New Century Financial Corporation, a large subprime mortgage lender, noted that 'KPMG's engagement team acquiesced in New Century's departures from prescribed accounting methodologies . . . at times the engagement team acted more as advocates for New Century, even when its practices were questioned.'[7] And the court-appointed examiner into the Lehman bankruptcy noted that Ernst & Young, Lehman's auditors, 'failed to question and challenge improper or inadequate disclosures'[8] in the firm's reports and accounts. In particular, they focused on the use of sale and repurchase transactions to move assets off-balance sheets at quarter end, the so-called Repo 105 transactions. The examiner notes, 'Ernst & Young took virtually no action to investigate the Repo 105 allegations . . . Ernst & Young took no steps to challenge the non-disclosure by Lehman of its use of $50 billion of temporary off-balance sheet transactions.' These claims are likely to be the subject of litigation.

In assessing the scope for improving the utility and relevance of external audit work, the UK Treasury Committee saw the most promising route as being through enhanced communication between auditors and regulators, where the former had concerns they wished to raise. They also argued for tighter rules on the independence of auditors, although those rules were significantly tightened, especially in the United States, after the Enron failure, without any noticeable effect on the propensity of auditors to challenge management.

Overall, the somewhat depressing conclusion, from the perspective of the audit profession itself, is that audit firms did not perform a useful role in highlighting the emergence of life-threatening risks in financial firms, but that most analysts and commentators think they are unlikely ever to do so, and that the weight that can be placed on audit opinions is not great.

The link between an unqualified audit opinion and corporate financial health is highly tenuous, at best. The conclusion reached by Sikka is that 'the current financial crisis is an opportunity to consider alternative institutional arrangements for auditing. Alternative models need not directly involve accounting firms and audits of banks could be conducted by statutory regulators. This would also improve banking regulators' knowledge of banks.'[9] That is not an encouraging prognosis for the accounting profession.

References

1. Financial Crisis and the Silence of the Auditors. Prem Sikka. *Accounting, Organizations and Society* 2009, Vol. 34.
2. Banking Crisis: Reforming Corporate Governance and Pay in the City. Report of the Treasury Committee, House of Commons. May 2009. www.publications.parliament.uk/
3. Oral Evidence on Auditors and Credit Rating Agencies, taken before the Treasury Committee. House of Commons. 28 January 2009. www.publications.parliament.uk/
4. Activity Report 2007. Financial Reporting Review Panel. www.frc.org.uk
5. Banking Crisis, Treasury Committee Report.
6. Ibid.
7. Final Report In re: New Century Trs Holdings. United States Bankruptcy Court for the District of Delaware. 2008. http://graphics 8.nytimes.com/
8. Report of the Examiner in the Chapter 11 proceedings of Lehman Brothers to the United States Bankruptcy Court for the Southern District of New York. Anton Valukas. 11 March 2010. http://lehman report.jenner.com/
9. Financial Crisis, Sikka.

23

CONFLICTS OF INTEREST CREDIT RATING AGENCIES

Credit rating agencies (CRAs) have existed for around 100 years. Their principal role is to give ratings to debt obligations which are intended to express their creditworthiness. The rating has a significant influence on the price of the debt. There are three large international agencies: Standard & Poors, Moody's and Fitch, together with a number of other more specialized firms. The ratings are widely used by investors and regulators. Many elements of capital regulation are built around them, with lower reserve ratios ascribed to holdings of 'investment grade' debt, typically rated BBB or above.

Before the crisis, the CRAs were not directly regulated outside the United States. In the United States they were obliged to register with the SEC as nationally recognized securities ratings organizations (NRSROs). That registration did not involve intrusive intervention by the SEC and there was no close oversight of the rating process. Following the Enron failure, when the company's debt was downgraded just hours before its collapse, there was considerable debate in the United States about the oversight of CRAs, and some legislative changes.[1]

The core business of the ratings agencies for many decades related to corporate bonds. But as the 'originate to distribute' model of bank credit extension developed, they also began to assign ratings to securitizations of various kinds. In 2007, this securitization rating business had come to account for around half of the revenues of main agencies. As a result, their business was remarkably profitable during this period. The agencies earned more for grading these complex products than they did in relation to corporate bonds.

Many of these securitizations were, with the assistance of insurance provided by monoline insurers, highly rated. Reflecting the insurance backing of the monolines, and the performance of mortgage pools through a period of rapidly rising house prices, the number of securitizations rated AAA grew rapidly. By the end of 2006, while there were only a dozen AAA rated corporates in the US market, it is estimated that there were only around 65,000 AAA rated securitization instruments. Some of these were known as CDOs squared, where the underlying asset of the securitization was BBB, but parts of it were converted into AAA securities through tranching and sometimes the addition of credit insurance.

When house prices levelled off at the end of 2006, and began to fall in 2007, the prices of these securitizations began to fall sharply, as the default rate of the underlying mortgages escalated. From the end of 2007, through to the middle of 2008, the ratings agencies lowered the credit ratings on almost $2 trillion of mortgage-backed securities. These downgrades contributed to further price falls. By the end of 2008, some of these AAA securities were trading at a small fraction of their nominal value.

As a result, the CRAs were widely criticized. It was argued that they had profited unreasonably from these markets, assigned excessively high ratings without due diligence, and by their actions, both in their initial ratings process and in the downgrades, had accentuated the boom and bust cycle. Joseph Stiglitz, among others, saw them as at the centre of the meltdown. He said, 'I view the rating agencies as one of the key culprits . . . they were the party that performed the alchemy that converted the securities from F rated to A rated. The banks could not have done what they did without the complicity of the ratings agencies.'[2]

In the period since the crisis erupted, this condemnation of the CRAs has been 'parsed' into a number of distinct charges. Four have assumed particular significance.

First, it is argued that the CRA business is subject to fundamental conflicts of interest. Until the early 1970s, the basic business model of ratings agencies depended on investors paying for ratings. But around the time of the bankruptcy of the Penn Central Railroad in 1970, the business model changed from an 'investor pays' system to an 'issuer pays' system, whereby the entity that is issuing the bonds also pays the rating firm to rate the bonds. That high profile bankruptcy 'made issuers more conscious of the need to assure bond investors that they [the issuers] really were low risk, and they were willing to pay the credit rating firms to have the latter option for them'. This payment model may be said to encourage the ratings agencies to be prepared to grant as high a rating as possible, in order to secure the business from the issuer.[3]

In the case of securitizations, the incentives are particularly strong. As Charles Goodhart has argued, 'with fees generally higher in relation to marginal costs, as is the case for a corporate rating, the incentive to overrate to secure a fee is that much greater (and the investment bankers proposing a deal can be demanding – they want their high bonuses for getting the issue away)'.[4] Internal documents published in April 2010 as part of a US Senate investigation showed that positive ratings were sometimes offered as part of the fee negotiation between issuers and CRAs, and that this trend was a matter of concern to some within the CRAs themselves.[5]

Second, it is argued that the relationship between issuers, often the investment banks, and the credit rating agencies, is different in the case of securitizations. The CRAs advise the issuers on how to structure the issue to achieve a desired rating. They earn fees for that consultancy function. This process raises doubts about the objectivity of the final rating process. Furthermore, the CRAs may not themselves have understood the business well enough. Willem Buiter has argued that they 'got into a line of business that they did not understand. They were reasonable at rating sovereign risk and large corporates but not at rating complex structures, but they did it anyway.'[6]

Third, there is some evidence that issuers may indulge in 'ratings shopping', whereby they will seek the highest available rating and choose that one only. While most companies want their corporate bonds to be rated by all the major agencies, structured issues are usually only rated by one or two of them. 'The proposers seek out the agency that will give the highest rating (or demand the least credit enhancement to achieve the desired ratings); the other agencies are then not used. That indicates a prima facie case for bias.'[7]

Fourth, it is argued that the agencies erred in using the same rating scale for securitizations that they used for corporate debt. There is evidence that the CRAs 'have done a reasonably good job of predicting the probability of default of corporate bonds relative to regulatory indicators of default risk and market measure of default risk'.[8] But this success was built on an extensive database of corporate bonds, and an assessment of default performance over a long period. There could be no similar record related to complex asset-backed securitizations, where the market had opened only recently. Using the scale applied to conventional corporate bonds therefore implied an equivalence between these two asset classes and their likely performance which could not be justified. As the crisis developed, it became clear that, at the very least, the volatility of prices of these assets was very different, especially in stressed liquidity conditions. The CRAs may therefore be criticized for misleading market participants in a manner which contributed materially to the crisis.

Fifth, in the summer of 2010, as the fiscal crisis hit Europe, it was argued that the rating agencies downgraded the government debt of affected countries, like Greece, in a way which contributed to the crisis. European politicians threatened retribution, and the creation of a European agency which, presumably, would behave in a more obliging manner.

At the same time, it was argued that a number of the problems arose from weaknesses and failures in the regulatory environment:

(1) The NRSRO framework was one of registration not regulation, and offered little in the way of comfort to investors about the way the agencies operated.
(2) The way the SEC managed the registration process effectively maintained an oligopoly. The NRSRO designation created in 1975 'subsequently became a barrier to entry into the ratings business'.[9] Twenty-five years later there were still only three regulated agencies.

(3) Regulators elsewhere compounded the problems by their extensive use of ratings in regulation. 'By outsourcing public authority to private firms, this practice intensifies the conflict of interest.'[10] The Basel II capital requirements framework (Section 7) magnified the problem by making much more extensive use of ratings than did its predecessor. This regulatory use encouraged investors to adopt ratings as a shorthand for risk assessment, essentially outsourcing their own credit appraisal to the CRAs.

The CRAs themselves have rejected much of this criticism. While accepting that there has been a loss of confidence in the credit rating process, they have defended the 'issuer pays' model. They argue that 'potential conflicts exist regardless of who pays. The key is how well the rating agencies manage the potential conflicts.'[11] They point out that investors, too, have an interest in the rating of a bond, just as the issuer does, even if that interest is the reverse. Investors frequently are also issuers, and in those cases the distinction between investor pays and issuer pays is not meaningful. So, in their view, the important point is how well conflicts are managed. They argue that they manage those conflicts in a variety of ways, including making decisions by committees rather than individual analysts, prohibiting analysts from holding fee discussions with issuers, compensating analysts in a manner unrelated to the revenue they earn from the entities they rate, etc. The Treasury Committee of the UK Parliament accepted this line of argument, recognizing 'that there are conflicts inherent in every payment model. It is our view that transparency offers the best available defence against conflicts of interest.'[12]

Nonetheless, the principal agencies have agreed with the New York State Attorney General to additional measures 'to limit perceived conflicts of interest and to curtail ratings shopping in the rating of subprime mortgage securitizations. The new agreement includes provisions requiring issuers to pay for the review of securities regardless of whether a rating ultimately is used.'[13] They have also accepted additional rules proposed by the SEC designed to 'foster increased transparency, accountability, and competition in the credit rating agency industry for the benefit of investors'.[14]

The agencies argue, however, that their opinions are subject to the privilege of free speech. They have therefore claimed first amendment protection against litigation seeking to establish liability in respect of ratings. The agencies assert that they have the same status as financial journalists, which 'precludes government regulation of the content of a rating opinion or the underlying methodology'.[15] They have been critical of a European directive to regulate ratings agencies, which establishes a supervisory structure for CRAs in Europe, making them 'subject to surveillance of the security supervisors that already oversee the EU's financial markets at national level'.[16] They point out that the fiscal problems of euro area members were well known, and that the risk of default was real. If they were prevented from downgrading vulnerable sovereign borrowers the interests of investors would be damaged.

The consequence of the crisis has, therefore, been a range of new regulatory measures aimed at introducing direct government oversight of the CRAs and at improving the integrity of the rating process, particularly for structured finance. Less progress has been made on introducing competition into the industry, or on reducing the significance of ratings in regulation. A World Bank study argues that 'reducing the hard wiring of rating agencies in regulatory frameworks is essential to minimize complacency among market participants and regulators'.[17] The Bank of England has signalled a move away from reliance on ratings in respect of the collateral it accepts in its operations.[18] But it is not easy for regulators to find an alternative globally accepted methodology to measure the relative default risk of different debt investments, which is an essential building-block of prudential regulation. So while regulators will, in future, have a better insight into the rating agencies, the fundamental conflicts of interest and incentives remain broadly as they were before the crisis.

References

1. *Global Financial Regulation: The Essential Guide.* Howard Davies and David Green. Polity Press. Cambridge. 2008.

2. Bringing Down Wall Street as Ratings Let Loose Subprime Scourge. Elliot Blair Smith. Bloomberg. 24 September 2008. www.bloomberg.com

3. The Credit Rating Agencies and the Subprime Debacle: Understanding Their Centrality and What to do About It. Lawrence White. FinReg21[beta]. 19 October 2009. www.finreg21.com

4. How, if at all, should Credit Ratings Agencies (CRAs) be Regulated? Charles Goodhart. Financial Markets Group Special Paper 181. June 2008. www.lse.ac.uk

5. Moody's and S&P were Unduly Influenced by Bankers, Probe Finds. Stephanie Kirchgaessner and Kevin Sieff. *Financial Times*. 23 April 2010. www.ft.com

6. Oral Evidence Ev88 – Banking Crisis Inquiry. Treasury Committee. 13 January 2009. www.publications.parliament.uk/

7. Summary Report of Issues Identified in the Commission Staff's Examinations of Select Credit Rating Agencies. US Securities and Exchange Commission. July 2009. www.sec.gov

8. The Financial Economists' Roundtable's Statement on Reforming the Role of SROs in the Securitisation Process. Charles Goodhart. 5 December 2008. http://voxeu.org

9. Credit Rating Agencies and The Next Financial Crisis – Testimony by Lawrence White. US House of Representatives' Oversight and Government Reform Committee. 24 September 2009. www.house.gov

10. Financial Economists' Roundtable's Statement, Goodhart.

11. Testimony by Raymond W. McDaniel. US House of Representatives' Oversight and Government Reform Committee. Subcommittee on Capital Markets, Insurance and Government-Sponsored Enterprises. 22 October 2008. www.house.gov

12. Banking Crisis: Reforming Corporate Governance and Pay in the City. Report of the Treasury Committee, House of Commons. May 2009. www.publications.parliament.uk/

13. Testimony by McDaniel.

14. SEC Proposes Comprehensive Reforms to Bring Increased Transparency to the Credit Rating Process. SEC Press Release. 11 June 2008. www.sec.gov

15. Credit Rating Agencies – No Easy Regulatory Solutions. Jonathan Katz et al. Crisis Response Note 8. The World Bank Group. October 2009. http://rru.worldbank.org

16. EU Credit Rating Agencies Proposal – briefing. EU Business News. 12 November 2008. www.eubusiness.com

17. Credit Rating Agencies, Katz et al.

18. Bank to Perform its Own Risk Assessment. Chris Giles. *Financial Times*. 17 March 2010. www.ft.com

E FINANCIAL FIRMS AND MARKETS

The macroeconomic environment may have been unstable, the regulations faulty, and the accountants and others ineffective, but the firms at the heart of the market failures made their own decisions, supposedly with the interests of shareholders uppermost. Why did many make such poor decisions?

One argument centres on the 'originate to distribute' model which collapsed in the subprime debacle, and which distanced borrowers from lenders and weakened normal market disciplines (Section 24). The products devised by inventive firms may have become too complex to be understood (25). Risk management did not keep pace with the speed of innovation (26). Boards of directors were especially weak in these circumstances, failing to understand the dynamics of the businesses they were supposed to oversee (27).

Other arguments focus on incentive structures. Were not individuals within banks incentivized precisely to take risk, for which they were handsomely rewarded in the short term, even if the firm and its shareholders subsequently paid a heavy price (28)? Might there not also have been fraudulent behaviour, with investment banks cynically exploiting other investors? (29).

And what of the rogue beasts in the financial jungle? Did not aggressive and predatory hedge funds contribute to the fiasco, especially armed with the technique of short-selling, which allowed them to profit from others' distress (30 and 31)?

24

BREAKING THE CHAIN ORIGINATE TO DISTRIBUTE

Subprime mortgages, and their close cousins ALT-A, are provided to borrowers who would not normally be regarded as creditworthy. Many of them were so-called Ninja loans, extended to people with no incomes, no jobs and no assets.

Subprime lending, or non-status lending as it is more usually known in the UK, has always existed. There will be borrowers whose employment, financial and family circumstances do not fit comfortably into standard credit scoring models, but who are nonetheless entitled to credit. What was striking in the US in the early years of this century was the rapid growth of the overall size of the market, of the subprime share of total mortgages extended, and of unusual securitization and secondary market mechanisms. Subprime mortgages were below 10 per cent of all mortgage originations until 2004, but then grew to 20 per cent of the market at the peak in 2006. By March 2007 the value of US subprime mortgages was estimated at $1.3 trillion, with over 7.5 million loans outstanding.

The market depended on continued rises in house prices, which had increased by over 120 per cent between 1997 and 2006. Many mortgages were issued at loan-to-value rates above 100 per cent, and the average duration was less than three years, as families frequently remortgaged in order to continue to make interest payments. That remortgaging process was possible because house prices continued to rise. The market was, it now seems, riddled with fraudulent practices, bad advice by mortgage brokers to their clients, and so-called predatory lending.

These mortgages, which might originally be financed by a local bank, were then typically packaged and sold on quickly. Investment banks developed a large-scale business in securitizing subprime mortgages. The securitization process allowed banks to construct assets of different quality. So, for example, a mortgage pool would be tranched so that the senior portions would be rated as AAA, with lower tranches rated less highly, down to the equity tranche which was often referred to as 'toxic waste'. The reason this could be done was that the losses on the pool were aggregated so that the first default in the pool was a charge on the holder of the equity tranche. The AAA holders would not incur losses until more than half the mortgages were in default. The prices of these tranches, and the returns on them, of course varied in proportion to their relative vulnerability to default.

In a further twist, the BBB tranches were used to construct additional securitizations, also then divided into tranches. These further securitizations were typically known as CDOs (Collateralized Debt Obligations) squared. With the addition of credit insurance from monoline insurers, it was possible to convert parts of the BBB tranche into a super senior AAA asset. Many investors did not fully understand that the underlying assets remained BBB in quality. Hedge funds which wished to short the market encouraged the creation of new CDOs precisely to allow them to bet against it. These tranches were sold on to investors around the world. Indeed the early subprime collapses were in continental Europe, where German banks and others were found to have invested heavily in assets whose quality deteriorated very sharply in early 2007.

In the early months of that year this money machine came to a grinding halt. House prices began to fall at the end of 2006 and the prices of mortgage bank securities fell very rapidly as default rate and repossessions escalated. Foreclosures grew by around 80 per cent in 2007 over the previous year, with an additional 80 per cent increase in 2008. By the autumn of 2009 over 40 per cent of all US mortgages were either delinquent or in foreclosure. Some of the AAA securitizations were close to worthless. The destruction of value for financial institutions and investors probably approached $1 trillion. At the other end of the chain many households found themselves with negative equity and subsequently homeless. A new phrase, 'jingle mail', was invented to describe the practice of borrowers simply dropping their keys through the letterbox of the mortgage broker and leaving town. The basic outline of this boom and bust is now well understood. But there remain unanswered questions. How could sophisticated investors, including some of the investment banks themselves, have convinced themselves that this party would go on indefinitely? Does the collapse demonstrate a fundamental flaw in what is known as the 'originate to distribute' model, whereby banks and investment banks extend credit, but with the clear intention of selling that credit on through the securitization.

Critics argue that the model is indeed broken.[1] It is argued that 'originating brokers had little incentive to perform due diligence and monitor borrowers' credit worthiness, as most of the subprime loans originated by brokers were subsequently securitized'.[2] Investors further along the chain knew little of the quality of the underlying assets, resting on the apparent security of the credit rating. Investment banks were happy to construct elaborate products and to match buyers and sellers, even though they harboured doubts about the quality of the underlying assets, and the complex dynamics of the instruments in question.

The securitization products were very difficult to value. Each structure is unique and complex calculations must be made, which many investors ignored. Transparency was also limited. And the apparent security offered by insurance proved illusory as the monolines themselves collapsed.

Three years into the crisis there are few signs of a revival of investor interest in complex securitizations built on mortgages. Optimists, like Ben Bernanke of the Federal Reserve, believe it may be possible to put the genie back in the bottle. He has remarked, 'these problems notwithstanding, the originate to distribute model has proven effective in the past and with adequate repairs could be so again in the future'.[3] Malcolm Knight, then the manager of the BIS, similarly argued, 'what needs to be done is to strengthen the underpinnings of the originate to distribute model, in particular by enhancing the information available to market participants, incentive structures, risk management practices and the use of credit ratings'.[4]

Martin Wolf, in the *Financial Times*, thinks it will be necessary to go further, and recommends that investment banks should be required to hold a portion of the securitizations they create.[5] Nouriel Roubini is doubtful about whether even that will work. 'Proposing that such institutions hold some of that risk does not seem to be a solution that will fully resolve the problems deriving from the wrong set of financial incentives.' He points out that investment banks 'did keep in a variety of forms a significant fraction of that credit risk on their balance sheet'.[6] Furthermore, obliging originators to hold some of the first loss tranche gives the originator an incentive to put more highly correlated credit together in the asset pool.[7]

For now, it is hard to see a set of circumstances in which mortgage-backed securitization will revive on a large scale. Some of the factors which facilitated it – notably the possibility of holding the securitizations in off-balance sheet vehicles without robust capital backing – are no longer available. The future problem seems likely to be more how to improve the availability of mortgage finance, than how to regulate a revival of subprime securitizations.

References

1. Seven Habits that Finance Regulators Must Acquire. Martin Wolf. 7 May 2008. *Financial Times*. www.ft.com
2. The Subprime Credit Crisis of 07. Michel Crouhy, Robert Jarrow and Stuart Turnbull. September 2007. www.bauer.uh.edu
3. Addressing Weaknesses in the Global Financial Markets. Ben Bernanke. Speech at the World Affairs Council. Richmond, Virginia. 10 April 2008. www.federalreserve.gov
4. Some Reflections on the Future of the Originate-to-Distribute Model in the Context of the Current Financial Turmoil. Malcolm Knight. Speech at the Euro 50 Group Roundtable. London. 21 April 2008. www.bis.org
5. Seven Habits, Wolf.
6. Ten Fundamental Issues in Reforming Financial Regulation and

Supervision in a World of Financial Innovation and Globalization. Nouriel Roubini. 31 March 2008. http://media.rgemonitor.com/

7. Sense and Nonsense in the Current Debate about Credit Derivatives. Ron Anderson. March 2009. www.lse.ac.uk

25

TOO COMPLEX TO TRADE DERIVATIVES

Section 24 explained the mechanisms operating in the sub-prime markets and ways in which elaborate securitization techniques magnified risk. A re-examination in the last three years of these structures, and others, has led to a general critique of the growing complexity of the financial system, and of some of the products traded within it. The two decades leading up to the crisis saw an explosion of innovation, and an exponential growth in the interconnectedness of financial firms, nationally and globally. Both of these trends were generally thought of as positive. Product innovation allowed risk to be 'sliced and diced' into discrete components, which could then be better matched to investors' preferences. The conventional wisdom, expressed by the IMF in April 2006, was that 'the dispersion of credit risk by banks to a broader and more diverse group of investors, rather than warehousing such risk on their balance sheets, has helped to make the banking and overall financial system more resilient . . . The improved resilience may be seen in fewer bank failures and more consistent credit provision. Consequently, the commercial banks, a core segment of the financial system, may be less vulnerable today to credit or economic shocks.'[1]

The inaccuracy of this prognosis, which was shared by many others, has led to new thinking. While, in principle, these new products allowed risk to be dispersed, there were two significant drawbacks. First, the products were highly complex and hard to understand, both in themselves and in terms of their interaction with other balance sheet risks. And, second, the growing complexity of financial networks made it difficult for regulators to understand where risks were held in the financial system, and the consequences of financial failure.

Jean-Pierre Landau of the Bank of France has developed a helpful taxonomy of complexity.[2] He identifies four main elements:

(1) The network of counterparties expanded in scale and complexity as techniques for dispersing risk became more sophisticated. Risks were perhaps more broadly spread but counterparty risk increased, with a negative impact on financial stability.

(2) Complexity led to a loss of information, in that the chain of tranching and distributing risks made the underlying assets and risks hard for even informed investors to understand.

(3) There was 'a profound uniformity in the approach to risk' and in the risk appetite of apparently diverse firms. This uniformity was destabilizing in that herd behaviour resulted in an asset price bubble and at times of stress there was a concerted rush for the exit.

(4) Most importantly, complexity resulted in an increase in overall uncertainty, in the Knightian sense.

Landau notes that this analysis, particularly of the financial network, draws on work by Andy Haldane at the Bank of England.[3] Haldane's conclusion is that complexity and homogeneity have produced a financial network which is at the same time both robust and fragile, where feedback effects under stress add to that fragility, where uncertainty in the pricing of assets causes seizures in markets and where common business and risk management strategies have made the whole system less resistant to disturbance. This diagnosis well describes the events of 2007–08.

In his review, Turner adds an additional argument. He notes that 'the very complexity of the mathematics used to measure and manage risk . . . made it increasingly difficult for top management and boards to assess and exercise judgement over the risks being taken.'[4] So some of the apparent checks and balances within firms did not operate effectively, and at the same time firms became excessively reliant on credit ratings, in the absence of a clear understanding of the risk characteristics of the complex products which some had themselves created. In his entertaining review of the crash, *The Big Short*, Michael Lewis illustrates that, in some cases, senior management in investment banks did not understand the risks their firms were running.[5]

This line of argument has led many to question the value of much financial innovation. Adair Turner has suggested that much of it may be 'socially useless'. Certainly, the implicit assumption adopted by regulators and central bankers in the past that any financial innovation which had the effects of making markets more complete, in the sense of increasing the sophistication with which claims could be traded, may well now be questionable. Perhaps, therefore, the previous presumption that innovation was permissible unless explicitly forbidden should be replaced by the presumption that new products are forbidden unless explicitly permitted. Paul Volcker has said that the only unambiguously positive financial innovation of the last quarter century is the ATM.

Robert Litan of the Brookings Institution strenuously rejects Volcker's charge:[6] 'I find that there is a mix between good and bad financial innovations, although on balance I find more good ones than bad ones.' In the 'good' category he includes asset-backed securities, interest rate swaps and credit default swaps, while recognizing that others which looked positive at inception were eventually abused.

Others are more cautious. Ben Bernanke has warned against seeing innovation as part of the problem leading to the crisis. 'I think that perception goes too far, and innovation, at its best, has been and will continue to be a tool for making our financial system more efficient and more inclusive.'[7] Others too have cautioned that healthy babies may be discarded with some undoubtedly dirty bath water, if regulators in future are too restrictive. There has been market resistance, too, to efforts to standardize products and require them to be traded on exchanges, thus increasing transparency.

For the time being, these arguments remain somewhat theoretical, as in the summer of 2010 the securitization markets remained almost entirely closed. Unless new forms of securitization are developed, credit is likely to be heavily constrained in the future. But new products may not exhibit the same complexity and opacity as they did in the early years of this century.

References

1. Global Financial Stability Report – Market Developments and Issues. International Monetary Fund. April 2006. www.imf.org
2. Complexity and the Financial Crisis. Jean-Pierre Landau. Speech at the Bank of France and the Deutsche Bundesbank Conference. Gouvieux-Chantilly. 8 June 2009. www.banque-france.fr
3. Rethinking the Financial Network. Andrew G. Haldane. Speech at the Financial Student Association, Amsterdam. April 2009.
4. The Turner Review: A Regulatory Response to the Global Banking Crisis. Financial Services Authority. March 2009. www.fsa.gov.uk
5. *The Big Short*. Michael Lewis. W. W. Norton & Company. London. 2010.
6. In Defense of Much, But Not All, Financial Innovation. Robert Litan. February 2010. www.brookings.edu
7. Financial Innovation and Consumer Protection. Ben Bernanke. Speech at the Federal Reserve System's Conference. Washington, DC. 17 April 2009. www.federalreserve.gov

26

DISASTER MYOPIA RISK MANAGEMENT

Why were banks taken by surprise by the market moves of 2007–08? Why did some of them lose such enormous sums as a result? Why did their risk management systems not give them a hint of trouble brewing, or tell them that they needed larger capital buffers? The lack of clear answers to these questions has caused many to conclude that there were fundamental flaws in the way banks managed their risks.

Value at Risk (VaR) models are by a distance the most widespread tool used by banks to model the risk in their folios. VaR models were developed in the 1980s, particularly at JP Morgan.[1] The aim was to produce a measure of the risk of loss on a specific portfolio of financial assets. For any particular portfolio, VaR calculates the loss that would be incurred in that portfolio in various market conditions. Typically it will use data from the previous year and produce a single number which would normally be the maximum loss which would be incurred on the portfolio 99 per cent of the time. Although the results may be collapsed into a single number, to risk managers VaR is a system. In banks the VaR number is calculated daily and reported to senior management. Following an SEC requirement that banks should publish a measure of the risk in their portfolio, it became the industry standard for risk disclosure and the Basel Committee validated its use for capital requirement purposes. The locus classicus describing the derivation and usage of VaR is *Value at Risk: The New Benchmark for Managing Financial Risk* by Philippe Jorion.[2]

For some time, banks and their regulators have recognized the deficiencies in VaR models. They depend on backward-looking data. The LTCM collapse, when the fund's portfolio suffered losses which its models regarded as at least 7-sigma events on successive days, demonstrated its weaknesses starkly. So regulators and banks supplemented value at risk with stress testing, in which the bank would assume various combinations of extreme events and stress its portfolio to assess the losses that would be incurred in those apparently unlikely circumstances.

But even this combination of techniques, informed by the problems of the past, was found seriously wanting in the crisis. As Andrew Haldane of the Bank of England has argued, 'risk management models have during this crisis proved themselves wrong in a more fundamental sense. They failed Keynes' test – that it is better to be roughly right than precisely wrong. With hindsight, these models were both very precise and very wrong.'[3]

Prominent critics of VaR like Nassim Nicholas Taleb of *Black Swan* fame[4] have long argued that the models would lead to disaster. His charge is that the models were essentially untested and built by non-traders. They amounted to 'charlatanism', in that they claim to estimate the risk of rare events, which is fundamentally impossible. They therefore gave false confidence to those who used them, and particularly to senior management, especially when sanctified by the regulators, and could be exploited by traders who would use them to rationalize their bets. As Simon Johnson and James Kwak point out, 'if common sense would lead a risk manager to crack down on a trader taking large, risky bets, then the trader is better off if the risk manager uses VaR instead'.[5] VaR, therefore, created an incentive to take excessive but remote risks and in effect led to excessive risk-taking and leveraging in financial institutions by focusing on the centre of the distribution of possible returns and ignoring the tails.

The defenders of VaR models, while they do not deny that they can be misused, nonetheless argue that they are, on balance, positive. They measure what they measure, no more, no less. They are limited in that they are bound to use observation of past market conditions and incorporate no forecast of the future. Nonetheless, they can provide early warning of trouble ahead. David Viniar, the Chief Financial Officer of Goldman Sachs, who reined back their exposure to mortgages in the US after examining their VaR indicators in 2006, says 'VaR is a useful tool. The more liquid the asset, the better the tool. The more history, the better the tool.'[6] But even supporters of VaR recognize that in the market conditions of late 2007 and 2008, when many instruments became wholly illiquid, the models broke down.

Stress-testing did little better. Haldane believes that it is attributable largely to what he describes as 'disaster myopia', in other words 'agents' propensity to underestimate the probability of adverse outcomes, in particular small probability events from the distant past'.[7] His analysis is that 'the credit crunch of the past 18 months is but the latest in a long line of myopia-induced disasters'. Even the stress tests which were mandated by regulators were heavily influenced by the economic and market circumstances of the time. During the decade of rapid economic growth which came to a shuddering halt in 2006, the distribution of outcomes for both microeconomic and financial variables was very different from what it has been over a much longer period. He points out that if the data in VaR calculation is extended for a year beyond mid-2007, the VaRs for UK banks increase on average by 60 per cent. So, on this analysis, the apparently complicated and mathematically sophisticated models used by banks are in effect simply the expression of a hope that the good times will continue to roll, and that financial markets will continue to behave in the future as they have in the past.

In spite of these stringent criticisms, and the experiences of the last two years, VaR models continue to be used by financial firms, albeit with some greater sophistication, more extensive qualifications around them when presented to senior management and the public, and typically accompanied by more aggressive stress tests than before. So the conventional VaR number is typically accompanied by a 'stressed VaR' calculation, which shows the potential portfolio loss in highly adverse market conditions. At present, the back testing includes the extravagantly bad market conditions of the last three years, which materially alters the numbers the models produce. In his critique of the crisis Alan Greenspan noted that the model collapsed because 'data input into the risk-management models generally covered only the past two decades, a period of euphoria. Had instead the models been fitted more appropriately to historic periods of stress, capital requirements would have been much higher and the financial world would be in far better shape today.'[8] If Greenspan is correct, VaR models and stress tests may prove more useful for the next few years, but their utility as guides to the future will inevitably deteriorate over time. Furthermore, stress testing is by its very nature ad hoc, and entirely dependent on the choice of scenarios made by firms or their regulators.

References

1. *Fool's Gold*. Gillian Tett. Little, Brown. 2009.
2. *Value at Risk: The New Benchmark for Managing Financial Risk*. Philippe Jorion. McGraw-Hill. 2006.
3. Why Banks Failed the Stress Test. Andrew Haldane. Bank of England. The Marcus-Evans Conference on Stress-Testing, 13 February 2009.
4. *The Black Swan*. Nassim Nicholas Taleb. Random House. 2007.
5. Seduced by a Model. Simon Johnson and James Kwak. 1 October 2009. http://economix.blogs.nytimes.com
6. Risk Mismanagement. Joe Nocera. *The New York Times*. 2 January 2009. www.nytimes.com
7. Why Banks Failed the Stress Test, Haldane.
8. The Financial Crisis and the Role of Federal Regulators – Hearing of Alan Greenspan. US House of Representatives' Committee on Oversight and Government Reform. 23 October 2008. www.house.gov

27

THE ROACH MOTEL CORPORATE GOVERNANCE

In October 2008, Alan Greenspan surprised his interlocutors in Congress by appearing to accept some responsibility for what had gone wrong, but his apology turned out not to speak to the Federal Reserve's monetary policy during his time of office, but rather to the way in which financial firms themselves had behaved. He said, 'those of us who have looked to the self-interest of lending institutions to protect shareholders' equity . . . are in a state of shocked disbelief'.[1] His description of the weaknesses of the governance of firms, and failure of the checks and balances within them designed to ensure safety and soundness, focused attention on the way shareholder interests had been represented. Ultimately, boards of directors are in the key fiduciary role in relation to shareholders, so their performance has been strongly criticized. Were they not among those who had been asleep at the switch in the run-up to the crisis?

The criticisms were loud on both sides of the Atlantic. The UK parliament's Treasury Committee, in a report on corporate governance and pay in the City,[2] said, 'the current financial crisis has exposed serious flaws and shortcomings in the system of non-executive oversight of bank executives in the banking sector. Too often, eminent and highly regarded individuals failed to act as an effective check on, and challenge to, executive managers, instead operating as members of a cosy club.' An OECD report[3] concluded 'that the financial crisis can be to an important extent attributed to failures and weaknesses in corporate governance arrangements which did not serve their purpose to safeguard against excessive risk-taking'.

In the US, corporate governance activist Nell Minow, the Editor of the Corporate Library, said, 'all the failures we are looking at now are the results of failures of those [strategy and risk management] tasks. The directors are entirely responsible.'[4] A report in *The Investment Professional*, the journal of a New York society of security analysts, was coruscating about the failure, and the reasons for it: 'a corporate board is a bit like a roach motel; once people are invited in they seldom choose to check out. That's why many boards still resemble the collection of cronies that were so common before SOX [the Sarbanes-Oxley Act] forced companies to appoint only independent directors to the nominating committee.'[5]

It is clear that boards of failed banks cannot hope to escape responsibility. In some cases, particularly in the UK, almost the entire boards of banks like Royal Bank of Scotland, Northern Rock and Lloyds have been replaced. But how far can the responsibilities for failure be laid at the door of the non-executive directors? What particular characteristics of boards were at fault, and is there anything which could be done, whether by legislators, regulators, or by boards themselves, to make non-executive oversight more effective? Some academics and commentators are highly sceptical about whether the non-executives on a board are ever likely to be an effective check or balance. How can independent non-experts, spending perhaps a day or two a month on the business, possibly hope to be a meaningful constraint on the ambitions of aggressive risk-taking managers?

Before considering those general questions, we should look at the specific criticisms levelled at corporate boards in respect of their performance before and during the crisis. We can subdivide the general assault on their performance into six particular charges:

(1) The non-executive (independent, in UK terminology) directors were the wrong people, with inadequate skills.
(2) They spent too little time on their responsibilities.

(3) They did not perform effective oversight of risk management.

(4) They placed excessive reliance on internal advice, and did not arm themselves with external, potentially contrary opinions.

(5) They constructed, or allowed to be constructed, compensation systems which drove dangerous risk-taking.

(6) The structure of boards in the US was fundamentally flawed, especially where the Chairman and Chief Executive were the same person.

The *first* point has been strongly made in relation to Lehman Brothers. According to *The Investment Professional*, 'at the time the venerable security firm collapsed, it had ten independent Directors, of whom nine were retirees, four were aged over 75 (including a theatrical producer who sat on both the Audit Committee and the Finance and Risk Committee), and one was a former Admiral who spent her Navy career in human resources and education. Only two had ever worked in financial services.'[6] The UK Treasury Committee identified a lack of banking experience among many members of the boards of failed British institutions. Financial firms themselves seem to have acknowledged this criticism in their behaviour post-crisis, where many of them have looked to appoint board members with relevant expertise, rather than simply eminent members of the community from areas remote from the financial world.

There is some academic evidence that expertise on boards is relevant to performance. One long-term study finds that, over ten years, 'firms with more experienced independent directors experience higher abnormal returns and consistently beat analysts' earnings forecasts'.[7] This report covers non-financial firms as well as banks and is focused on stock market returns, rather than safety and soundness considerations. Another study, however, provides more direct evidence in relation to performance during the financial crisis. A study entitled 'Board (In)Competence and the Subprime Crisis' by three German academics[8] reviews the losses in German Landesbanken and relates them to an index of what they describe as 'boardroom competence', which includes educational background, financial experience, and management experience. Their sample covers the twenty-nine largest German banks. And their conclusion is that 'German banks with more competent supervisory members suffered smaller losses in the subprime crisis'.

A study of twenty-five European banks by Nestor Advisors[9] found that there was a link between failure and the type of independent directors on the board, though not with their number. But the relationships are relatively weak. They found that 'bank boards led by financial industry experts are likely to do a better job than by boards that are led by independent non-expert chairs', though there was a limited relationship in Europe between share price performance and factors such as board size, director independence, tenure, age, and expertise. A related study in the US, however, found that 'some of the more spectacular blow-ups of the last two years took place at banks where the average age and tenure of non-executive directors were far in excess of those displayed by their counterparts in the European banks'.[10] The US study is based on a small sample of six institutions, including the two which failed most comprehensively, Bear Stearns and Lehman Brothers. Nestor Advisors find that their boards had longer tenure, higher average age, and a smaller number of financial industry experts than those which survived. These conclusions are suggestive, but not conclusive. Overall, Nestor Advisors suggest that 'the best performers were the ones that followed a via media – boards that were not too young and had non-executive directors with mildly longer than average tenures', though they do point to the significance of financial industry expertise on the part of the chairman of the board.

However competent and experienced they may be, non-executive directors are unlikely to be effective if they spend too little time on the job. The *second* criticism has been in that area. In his review for the British government,[11] David Walker argued that the 'principal deficiencies in [financial industry] boards related much more to patterns of behaviour than to organization' and recommended 'a materially increased time commitment from the NED group on the board overall, for which a combination of financial industry experience and independence of mind will be much more relevant than a combination of lesser experience and formal independence.' His initial recommendation was that non-executive directors should commit no less than thirty-six days a year to their board duties. That proved controversial. Critics argued that this would almost certainly militate against recruiting to boards people with current financial industry experience. His final recommendation argued for differentiation, with some NEDs, especially with key committee responsibilities, spending 30–36 days a year, while others might have a lesser commitment.

While a relationship between input and effectiveness might seem intuitively plausible, there is little hard evidence to suggest that a simple increase in time commitment would produce a more effective set of checks and balances on the executive. The crucial factor is what is done during the time spent, and how effective the challenge process is. In practice, the time commitments of non-executive directors of banks have risen significantly in the last two years, as evidenced by the increases in the numbers of meetings of audit and risk committees. It remains to be seen whether this increased time commitment translates into more effective oversight.

The *third* criticism relates to the effectiveness of the oversight of risk management. Some banks have operated with separate risk committees. In other cases, risk oversight has been one of the functions of the audit committee. Most banks are now separating that role and such a separation is effectively mandated in the UK by the inclusion of the Walker Review recommendation in the Corporate Governance Code. Walker argues that every large financial firm should have a separate risk committee with 'responsibility for oversight and advice to the board on the current risk exposures of the entity and future risk strategy'. The committee should also take account of the macroeconomic and financial environment and the advice given by central banks and regulators on emerging risks to financial stability.

Financial regulators and others have argued that 'boards fail to understand and manage risk'.[12] A group of senior supervisors from regulatory agencies in several countries identified 'the unwillingness or inability of boards of directors . . . to articulate, measure and adhere to a level of risk acceptable to the firm' as one of the contributory factors leading to the breakdown.[13]

The *fourth* point is that boards of directors have tended to rely almost exclusively on internal sources of information, apart from the services of the external auditors, but the value added of external auditors in relation to prospective management of risk is generally acknowledged to be low. The absence of external perspectives limits the ability of the independent directors to challenge the executive, but the question of whether they should take external advice is controversial. Opponents see the risk that external advisers cut across the firm's own risk management procedures and might therefore have the effect of reducing management discipline. Others argue that an external check or balance can only be useful. In his review, David Walker sits on the fence, recommending that 'the board risk committee should be attentive to the potential added value from seeking external input to its work as a means of taking full account of relevant experience elsewhere and in challenging its analysis and assessment'.

The *fifth* area in which it is argued that boards were found wanting is in the design of compensation structures. Did boards oversee compensation arrangements which encouraged reckless and excessive risk-taking and which were not aligned with the interests of shareholders and the long-term sustainability of the banks? Boards are ultimately responsible for compensation. National supervisors, and the Financial Stability Board, have questioned whether the compensation and incentive structures were appropriate. The UBS report on its catastrophic losses accepted that the compensation structures there meant that bonuses were measured against gross revenue with no formal account taken of the quality or sustainability of earnings.[14] But the extent to which compensation failings were contributors to the breakdown remains controversial. It is discussed further in Section 28.

The *sixth* point is that board structure was at fault. Critics of US boards tend to argue that there is a need for a split between the Chairman and the Chief Executive roles to ensure greater discipline on the executive from a board led by a Chairman who is not a full-time executive. Canadian boards tend to follow the UK model of a split Chair and Chief Executive, whereas many European bank boards, notably in Germany, either follow a UK model or have a supervisory board above the executive management. Only a few US institutions (but now including Bank of America and Morgan Stanley) have divided the roles.

Unfortunately, it is hard to identify a clear relationship between board structure and success. UK banks, as a generality, suffered as badly as their transatlantic counterparts. The report by Nestor Advisors on European banks offers only the conclusion that 'boards led by financial industry experts are likely to do a better job than boards who are led by independent non-expert chairs'. This tends to point to a case for elevating Chief Executives to the Chairman's suite, as both HSBC and Standard Chartered have done in the UK. Those banks seemed to perform better in the crisis than others who had followed the pure milk of the UK corporate governance doctrine, which counsels against a Chairman who was formerly the CEO. But, of course, there may be other explanations for the relative success of those two banks, relating to the business models they operated, rather than to their risk management structures. There is no clear evidence on that point.

A broad conclusion from external analysis, and from some self-examination within bank boards, is that the level of financial expertise on boards ought to rise, that there may be a case (which would again be inconsistent with the UK Corporate Governance Code) for longer terms of service on bank boards to allow for the development of appropriate expertise, that risk committees separate from audit committees are likely to be appropriate in the future, and that non-executive independent board members will have to spend more time on their board responsibilities in future.

This does not sound like a revolution in the boardroom. Does that matter?

Some would argue that there are severe limitations on the abilities of boards dominated by non-executives to carry out effective oversight. As one UK commentator has suggested, the shortcomings of corporate governance have been so severe that 'one wonders if they can ever be solved. Might it not be easier to make the banks smaller and simpler, rather than look for a legion of superheroes to run them?'[15]

In the UK, as the Treasury Select Committee noted, 'both Lord Turner [of the FSA] and the Governor of the Bank of England were sceptical of the claim that more effective non-executive directors could have prevented the current banking crisis or was the key factor in averting future crises'.[16] Adair Turner argued that regulatory changes were more likely to decrease the likelihood of systemic crisis in the future 'than operating through the competence of the executives or the non-executives of specific institutions'. Paul Myners, the Treasury Minister in the Brown government with the responsibility for financial services, placed more emphasis on the need for reform in banks' corporate governance, and the government endorsed the recommendations of the Walker Review which, if fully implemented, would have significant implications for the nature of the non-executive role. But it is difficult to see a justification for placing much greater reliance on boards, primarily composed of part-time independent directors, in bolstering defences against future bouts of severe financial instability.

References

1. The Financial Crisis and the Role of Federal Regulators – Hearing of Alan Greenspan. US House of Representatives' Committee on Oversight and Government Reform. 23 October 2008. www.house. gov
2. Banking Crisis: Reforming Corporate Governance and Pay in the City. Report of the Treasury Committee, House of Commons. May 2009. www.publications.parliament.uk/
3. The Corporate Governance Lessons from the Financial Crisis. Grant Kirkpatrick. OECD Working Paper. 2009. www.oecd.org/daf/ corporateaffairs
4. Asleep at the Switch? Corporate Boards' Culpability in the 2008 Financial Crisis. Neil O'Hara. *The Investment Professional*, Vol. 2, No. 3. Summer 2009. www.theinvestmentprofessional.com
5. Ibid.
6. Ibid.
7. Boards of Directors: The Value of Industry Experience. Filippos Papakonstantinou. Working Paper. Imperial College London. November 2007.

8. Board (In)competence and the Subprime Crisis. Harald Hau *et al.* *Vox.* 12 January 2009. www.voxeu.org
9. Bank Boards and the Financial Crisis – A Corporate Governance Study of the 25 Largest European Banks. David Ladipo and Stilpon Nestor. Nestor Advisors. May 2009. www.nestoradvisors.co.uk
10. Governance in Crisis: A Comparative Case Study of Six US Investment Banks. NeAd Research Note 0109. April 2009. www. nestoradvisors.co.uk
11. A Review of Corporate Governance in UK Banks and other Financial Industry Entities. David Walker. 26 November 2009. www.hm-treasury.gov.uk
12. Second Statement on the Financial Crisis. International Corporate Governance Network. March 2009. www.icgn.org
13. Risk Management Lessons from the Global Banking Crisis of 2008. Senior Supervisors Group reporting to the Financial Stability Board, Bank for International Settlements. 2009. www.financialstability board.org
14. Shareholder Report on UBS's Write-Downs. April 2008. www.ubs. com
15. In the Banks, the Mavericks Survived. Anthony Hilton. *London Evening Standard.* 5 May 2009. www.thisislondon.co.uk/
16. Banking Crisis, Treasury Committee Report.

28

BLANKFEIN'S BONUS PAY AND INCENTIVES

The question of how far bankers' pay drove the behaviour which led to the crisis has been one of the most controversial. Intriguingly, corporate pay is known as remuneration on the eastern side of the Atlantic, while in the west it is deemed to be 'compensation', a subtle terminological shift which implies payoff for some unpleasant task which disrupts an otherwise happy and peaceful life. This beguiling use of language has not, however, insulated American bankers from public and political hostility to the large size of their pay packages.

Some of the anger has focused simply on the scale of reward to senior bankers. Lloyd Blankfein of Goldman Sachs was paid $68m for 2006. Rewards for senior executives, and especially bankers, have escalated in recent decades in relation to pay in the US and UK economies as a whole. Is this attributable to weaknesses in competition, or flaws in industrial structure? Are investment banks in practice able to trade on inside information, even if not technically guilty of regulatory offences? Or is it a problem of asymmetric information? The last theory has been advanced persuasively by Paul Woolley of the LSE.[1]

There is also a separate inflammatory question about the extent to which investment banks, in particular, were able to profit from the loose liquidity conditions and cheap money in the post-crisis period, as central banks put the economy on life support. It was argued that those who had done most to precipitate the crisis were then benefiting most from the necessary response to it. But these arguments did not address the central question of the extent to which the incentive structures in place in financial institutions drove risk-taking behaviour which itself generated asset price bubbles and financial instability.

The argument advanced in favour of this view was that Chief Executives, and indeed traders in banks, are typically rewarded on the basis of short-term performance. They may therefore have an incentive to take on risky positions which yield high immediate returns. Those returns may well be enhanced greatly by leverage. But, as the meltdown showed, those profits may prove to be illusory. The positions banks took on which showed a profit in early 2007 generated massive losses just a few months later. In the meantime, the traders had taken, and possibly spent, their cash bonuses, or indeed offloaded their shares or options. Then the shareholders, and also the taxpayers, were left to cope with the consequences. This argument has been widely canvassed by politicians in many countries, by commentators and even by regulators. So, for example, Tim Geithner, the US Treasury Secretary, told Congress that 'what happened to compensation and the incentives in creative risk-taking did contribute in some institutions to the vulnerability that we saw in this financial crisis'.[2] What evidence is there to support this contention?

The studies which have attempted to answer this question have so far focused primarily on Chief Executives' pay, where the data is largely in the public domain. Less analysis has been done on the implications of incentive structures on particular trading desks, where there is anecdotal evidence to suggest that some traders may have taken risks of which even their senior management was unaware. But as far as the CEOs are concerned the evidence of a relationship between incentive structures and unwise risk-taking seems weak. In a paper on bank CEO incentives and the credit crisis Fahlenbrach and Stulz[3] say, 'there is no evidence that banks with CEOs whose incentives were better aligned with the interests of their shareholders performed better during the crisis and some evidence that these banks actually performed worse, both in terms of stock returns and in terms of accounting return on equity'. The CEOs of the banks which failed did not cut their shareholdings in anticipation of or during the crisis. So the most well-publicized failures, such as Bear Stearns or Lehman Brothers, were also catastrophic for the net worth of their Chief Executives, Jimmy Cayne and Dick Fuld. (Curiously, another paper, by Yermack and Liu, does find a negative relationship between CEOs' purchase of extravagant homes and company performance: 'future company performance deteriorates when CEOs acquire extremely large or costly mansions or estates'.[4])

In his review of the crisis, Adair Turner reaches a similar conclusion. He notes that while there is 'a strong prima-facie case that inappropriate incentive structures played a role in encouraging behaviour which contributed to the crisis . . . a reasonable judgement is that while remuneration structures played a role, they were considerably less important than . . . inadequate approaches to capital, accounting and liquidity'. His conclusion was that excessive risk-taking, at least at the top level of management, 'may be driven more by broad behavioural and cultural factors than by a rational consideration of the precise incentives inherent within remuneration contracts: dominant executive personalities have a strong tendency to believe in their own strategies'.[5]

Others do not accept this interpretation of events. Bebchuk and Spamann of Harvard believe that even if, ex post, CEOs did not profit substantially from excessive risk-taking, bankers' incentives did matter. Even if the executives suffered large losses 'this does not mean that, ex ante, these executives had optimal incentives to prevent their banks from taking excessive risks'. They argue that there was an asymmetry inherent in strategies built on measurements of the performance of common stock, which is the principal currency of executive reward. Excessive risk-taking may in the short term bid up the price of common stock, while leaving other stakeholders, notably bondholders, exposed to subsequent losses. Bebchuk and Spamann therefore argue that bank executives expect to share in gains to common shareholders but are insulated from losses to bondholders, depositors and taxpayers, and therefore 'have incentives to give insufficient weight to the downside of risky strategies'. They argue that 'to encourage more prudent decision making, bank executives' equity based compensation could be replaced with compensation based on the value of a broader basket of securities, including bonds, representing a larger part of the corporate pie'. They believe that, in future, regulators must take a much closer interest in pay structures within firms and their impact on incentives.[6]

Another recent study by Cheng, Hong and Scheinkman[7] took a somewhat longer perspective, looking at the pay structures of firms over a period, identifying those which appeared to pay significantly more than might be justified by their long-term performance. They found 'substantial heterogeneity in financial firms in which high compensation, high risk-taking and tail performance go hand in hand'. Among the consistent high payers in their sample were Bear Stearns, Lehman Brothers, Countrywide and AIG. They note that 'the aggressive firms that were yesterday's heroes when the stock market did well can easily be today's outcasts when fortunes reverse'. But they also note that there are cultural factors at work here, and that these more aggressive risk-taking structures may well simply reflect investors' preferences. Certain firms have more of a culture of high powered incentives and risk-taking and particular types of investor are attracted onto the stock registers of those firms. On this analysis, you 'pays your money and you takes your choice'.

And another Harvard study by Bebchuk et al.[8] points out that the senior executives of the failed firms cashed in large sums in supposedly performance-based compensation between 2003 and 2008, compensation that was not clawed back when the firms collapsed: 'overall, we estimate that the top executive teams of Bear Stearns and Lehman Brothers derived cash flows of about $1.4 billion and $1 billion respectively from cash bonuses and equity sales during 2000–2008'. It is therefore 'not possible to rule out, as standard narratives suggest, that the executives' pay arrangements provided them with excessive risk-taking incentives'.

Whatever the evidence shows, bankers' pay has become a matter of regulatory interest. Under the auspices of the G20, the Financial Stability Board has set out guidelines for compensation in banks in the future.[9] They have required banks to introduce longer-term pay arrangements, including clawback mechanisms which allow them to adjust returns in the light of the behaviour of positions over a longer horizon. Those guidelines are being implemented by regulators around the world. In addition, public pressure and changes in tax systems have contributed to significant reductions in the absolute levels of payouts, at least in the short term, though pay in the financial sector remains remotely high.[10] Turner argues that large increases in capital, particularly held against the trading book, will reduce the profitability of these activities in the future, and therefore the remuneration of those involved in them. But it will take some time to observe that impact. And, for the foreseeable future, bankers' pay is likely to remain an issue of lively public and political interest.

References

1. An Institutional Theory of Momentum and Reversal. Paul Woolley and Dimitri Vayanos. Financial Markets Group Discussion Paper 621. November 2008. www.lse.ac.uk
2. Short-Term Thinking Linked to Compensation Problems. Real Time Economics Blog. *The Wall Street Journal*. 29 September 2009. http://blogs.wsj.com
3. Bank CEO Incentives and the Credit Crisis. Rüdiger Fahlenbrach and Rene Stulz. NBER Working Paper 15212. July 2009. www.nber.org
4. Where Are the Shareholders' Mansions? CEOs' Home Purchases, Stock Sales, and Subsequent Company Performance. October 2007. Crocker Liu and David Yermack. Available at http://ssrn.com
5. The Turner Review: A Regulatory Response to the Global Banking Crisis. Financial Services Authority. March 2009. www.fsa.gov.uk
6. Regulating Bankers' Pay. Lucian Bebchuk and Holger Spamann. *Georgetown Law Journal*. Forthcoming, 2010.
7. Yesterday's Heroes: Compensation and Creative Risk-Taking. Ing-Haw Cheng, Harrison Hong and Jose Scheinkman. Unpublished Working Paper. Princeton University. October 2009. www.princeton.edu
8. The Wages of Failure: Executive Compensation at Bear Stearns and Lehman 2000–2008. Lucian Bebchuk, Alma Cohen, and Holger Spamann. Harvard Law School Discussion Paper No. 657. February 2010. www.law.harvard.edu/

9. Principles for Sound Compensation Practices. Financial Stability Board. 25 September 2009. www.financialstabilityboard.org
10. Bankers' Pay and Extreme Wage Inequality in the UK. Brian Bell and John Van Reenen. CEP Special Report. April 2010. www.cep.lse.ac.uk

29

THE VAMPIRE SQUID FRAUD

When the Queen opened a new building at the London School of Economics in November 2008 she was given a presentation on the crisis and its origins by Professor Luis Garicano. Her response was brief, and to the point: 'that's awful. Why did no one see it coming?' Garicano's response was that 'at every stage someone was relying on somebody else and everyone thought they were doing the right thing'. The answer was subsequently amplified in a letter to the Queen by a number of academics from the LSE and elsewhere.[1]

But there is another less charitable explanation of the actions of many in the financial sector. Nouriel Roubini says 'thanks to everything from warped compensation structures to corrupt agencies, the global financial system rotted from the inside out. The financial crisis merely ripped the sleek and shiny skin off what had become, over the years, a gangrenous mess.'[2] He is not the only one to argue that there must, surely, have been fraud and malfeasance at the heart of what the financial firms at the centre of the crisis were doing.

Goldman Sachs became the lightning rod for these criticisms, perhaps partly because of their conspicuous success. Unlike most of their competitors, they sailed through the crisis years with just one quarter of losses. Roubini attributes that success largely to 'upwards of $60b in direct and indirect help' from the federal government. In particular 'it was saved during the bail out of AIG, netting a cool $12b from taxpayers'. A celebrated article in *Rolling Stone* magazine was more vividly uncomplimentary, describing the firm as 'a great vampire squid wrapped around the face of humanity, relentlessly jamming its blood funnel into anything that smells like money'.[3]

But as the crisis rolled forward, for almost three years no specific charges were laid against investment banks or hedge funds. That changed abruptly in April 2010, when the SEC accused Goldman Sachs of fraud.[4] The essence of the charge was that in one transaction the selection of the bonds which formed the asset base of a CDO was influenced by John Paulson, a hedge fund manager who correctly called the turn in the mortgage market and profited extraordinarily as a result. Paulson helped to construct an investment he intended to short. Goldman Sachs did not, according to the SEC, disclose this involvement to the investors. The firm has strenuously denied the charge.

A court finding that the transaction was fraudulent would have serious consequences. Other cases would certainly follow, and may in any event. The SEC papers have already exposed market practices to a hostile gaze. The transaction was constructed essentially to respond to a hedge fund's desire to short the market rather than to hedge risks which already existed. Is this activity, known as 'reverse inquiry' business, in any way worthwhile? The end results were payments of $150 million from a German bank (rescued by German taxpayers) and $850 million from Royal Bank of Scotland (rescued by British taxpayers) to an über-rich speculator in New York. Internal emails released by a Senate inquiry showed that managers within Goldman had serious doubts about the investments they were creating. The Goldman Sachs role was also difficult to present as consistent with its self-proclaimed client focus. In the *Financial Times* John Gapper noted that Goldman can argue that it owed no fiduciary duty to IKB, but 'in the end, that is not good enough, certainly not for a bank which takes pride in putting clients first'.[5]

References

1. Letter to HM the Queen. Tim Besley and Peter Hennessy after a seminar at the British Academy. www.britac.ac.uk
2. *Crisis Economics*. Nouriel Roubini and Stephen Mihm. Penguin. New York 2010.
3. The Great American Bubble Machine. Matt Taibbi. *Rolling Stone*. 2 July 2009. www.rollingstone.com
4. SEC Accuses Goldman of Fraud in Housing Deal. Louise Story and Gretchen Morgenson. *The New York Times*. 17 April 2010. www.nytimes.com
5. Greed is not Good for Goldman. John Gapper. *Financial Times*. 22 April 2010. www.ft.com

30

A PLAGUE OF LOCUSTS
HEDGE FUNDS

Hedge funds have long been controversial beasts in the financial jungle. The term 'hedge fund' is not amenable to precise definition, but is used broadly to describe unregulated investment funds which operate a range of investment strategies including short-selling. The capital in the funds comes from a range of sources including wealthy individuals, university endowment funds and, increasingly, other investment funds which devote a share of their assets to so-called 'alternative asset managers' which is another term frequently used to describe hedge funds. The former Chairman of the Social-Democratic Party of Germany, Frank Müntefering, described them as 'swarms of locusts',[1] which reflects the way in which they are viewed by some politicians in continental Europe and in South East Asia.

Hedge funds have been identified as key participants in a succession of financial crises, from the Asian episode in the late 1990s through the dot-com boom and bust, and into the subprime and broader financial crisis of 2007–2009. As Maria Stromqvist of the Swedish Central Bank notes in 'Hedge Funds and Financial Crises',[2] 'a discussion of the impact of hedge funds on the crisis is a recurring feature of every financial crisis. Even though the course of events in previous crises may have been very different, the criticism of hedge funds tends to be the same.'

After the Asian financial crisis, a review of hedge funds and the appropriate regulation thereof was carried out by a group under the auspices of the (then) Financial Stability Forum (the group was chaired by this author). The report,[3] which was subsequently twice updated, broadly concluded that insofar as hedge funds posed a risk to financial stability, that risk came through the addition of high leverage to their portfolios, and that leverage was provided by banks and investment banks. The most appropriate form of regulation of those funds was, therefore, indirect, operating through the exercise of control on banks' leverage and where it went. So while there was an argument for regulators to know more about what hedge funds were doing, in pursuit of their general market oversight responsibilities, the case for prudential regulation of funds was not made out.

In practice, over the last decade, different jurisdictions have handled hedge funds in different ways. Broadly, one might say that the US authorities have been reluctant to enter into any direct relationship with funds, although more recently the SEC has been prepared to do so. In the UK, hedge fund managers are typically regulated by the Financial Services Authority, and have generally found that relationship to be useful. The funds themselves, however, have usually been located in offshore jurisdictions, for a combination of reasons including taxation. Continental European regulators have broadly operated with the same approach, though relatively few hedge funds are headquartered in continental Europe, except in Switzerland, which has been somewhat more liberal than the UK. There are instances of hedge fund managers who have fallen foul of the regulators in the United Kingdom being allowed to set up funds in Switzerland.

But there has been no settled consensus on how the financial authorities should relate to hedge funds, and in the language of some continental Europeans, they have been seen as dark and opaque. The Italian Treasury Minister, Giulio Tremonti, has called for new regulations which should target 'absolutely crazy bodies, like hedge funds which have absolutely nothing to do with capitalism'.[4] Some of the concerns expressed by continental European politicians have been related to issues other than financial stability. There have been criticisms of the role hedge funds have played in takeover attempts. One episode, which attracted much criticism in Germany, was the failed merger between Deutsche Borse and the London Stock Exchange, where it was argued that hedge funds were a disruptive influence on corporate governance in continental Europe.[5]

Hedge fund critics also noted that the industry was growing very rapidly. Definitional problems make it hard to produce accurate estimates but, in round figures, assets under management probably grew from $500 billion to $2 trillion. The hedge funds point out that the assets under management remain very small by comparison with pension funds, mutual funds or insurance companies. These comparisons, however, ignore the different investment strategies available to these different types of institutions. Hedge funds, which are not required to follow index performance, and are unconstrained by prudential regulation, have far more freedom to take speculative positions and to trade actively during periods of market instability.

In the run-up to the London G20 meeting in 2009, the Germans hosted a European Summit in Berlin which focused attention on hedge funds and their role in the crisis. The statement issued after the meeting concluded that 'all financial markets, products and participants must be subject to appropriate oversight or regulation, without exception regardless of their country of domicile. This is especially true for those private pools of capital, including hedge funds, which may present a systemic risk'.[6] In the London and subsequent summits, Chancellor Merkel and President Sarkozy continued to press for further regulation of the hedge fund sector. After some reluctance from the European Commissioner responsible for financial market oversight, Charlie McCreevy, the Commission proposed a directive which would require hedge funds operating in European markets to register with local regulators in each case, unless they were subject to equivalent oversight in their home jurisdiction[7] (something that would not currently be the case in the United States). That directive prompted a critical letter from Treasury Secretary Geithner to Commissioner Barnier in March 2010, which exposed the different approaches taken in Europe and the US in this question.[8]

How far can hedge funds be said to have contributed to the crisis? Were they material influences on the instability of 2007–2009, as argued by the French and German governments?

Most in-depth reviews of the causes of the crisis have not identified hedge funds as prime suspects. The Swedish Central Bank review concludes that 'the claim that hedge funds in general have a greater impact on financial crises than other investors is not supported by the analysis here'.[9] The review notes that they have lost, as an asset class, considerable sums in the crisis and were affected disproportionately by the short-selling ban. The Turner Review notes that hedge fund leverage is typically well below that of banks and they do not perform a maturity transformation function 'fully equivalent to that performed by banks, investment banks, SIVs and mutual funds in the run-up to the crisis'.[10] Neither the de Larosière report for the European Union,[11] nor indeed the report commissioned by President Sarkozy himself by René Ricol,[12] gave hedge funds a starring role.

But while the case for a specific prudential regime for hedge funds has not been widely supported, as Turner suggests, 'hedge fund activity in aggregate can have an important pro-cyclical systemic impact. The simultaneous attempt by many hedge funds to deleverage and meet investor redemptions may well have played an important role over the last six months in depressing securities prices in a self-fulfilling cycle. And it is possible that hedge funds could evolve in future years, in their scale, their leverage and their customer promises, in a way which made them more bank-like and more systemically important.'[13]

A similar argument was advanced by Andrew Lo of MIT in his evidence to Congress on 'Hedge Funds, Systemic Risk and the Financial Crisis of 2007–2008'.[14] Lo argues that 'the dynamic and highly competitive nature of hedge funds also implies that their [investors] will shift their assets tactically and quickly, moving into markets when profit opportunities arise, and moving out when those opportunities have been depleted. Although such tactics benefit hedge fund investors, they can also cause market dislocation in crowded markets with participants that are not prepared for or fully aware of the crowdedness of their investments.' So, on this analysis, hedge funds may well have played a role in contributing to the liquidity crisis of 2007–08.

The Group of thirty report[15] in 2009 also identified this potentially destabilizing feature of hedge funds. The G30 raised another problematic issue. In a number of cases, investment banks either owned hedge fund managers outright, or had significant participations in them. Volcker argues that this cross-investment could itself generate systemic risk, and potentially expose the financial authorities, which since the autumn of 2008 effectively stand behind investment banks, to the risk of having to bail out institutions as a result of potential losses on their hedge fund investments. This led him to take the view that investment banks should be prohibited from taking proprietary positions in hedge fund groups, which became part of the proposed Volcker rule.

Turner concluded that while it was difficult to argue that hedge funds had played an important role in the most recent crisis, regulators and central banks needed much more extensive information on hedge fund activities in order to carry out their financial stability oversight role. Furthermore, regulators need the power to apply appropriate prudential regulation, 'if at any time they judge that the activities have become bank-like in nature or systemic in importance'.[16]

This approach may well, however, not satisfy the most outspoken critics. Hedge funds were once again seen as villains in the spring of 2010 when the credit default swap spreads on Greek sovereign debt widened dramatically, while concerns in the market rose about the sustainability of the country's fiscal position. It was argued that hedge funds were seeking to 'pick off' one weak country after another to make a killing. The evidence for large-scale hedge fund activity in this market was not overwhelming, but while their activities remain opaque, it is likely that they will come in for continued criticism of this kind. Over time, it seems inevitable that the financial authorities will need more visibility of hedge fund trading patterns and more direct observation of their leverage, even though the retrospective analysis suggests that, after peaking in 2001, hedge fund leverage remained modest in the run-up to the crisis. If leverage was the principal culprit, hedge funds were only modest accessories to the crime.

References

1. The Day of the Locusts. Peter Gumbel. *Time.* 15 May 2005. www. time.com
2. Hedge Funds and Financial Crises. Maria Strömqvist. Sveriges Riksbank *Economic Review* No. 1/2009. 2009. www.riksbank.com
3. Report of the Working Group on Highly Leveraged Institutions. Financial Stability Forum. March 2000. www.financialstabilityboard. org
4. Italy's Call to Abolish Hedge Funds Resisted. Daniel McAllister. Financial Adviser. 20 October 2008. www.ftadviser.com
5. Hedge Funds Derailed Deutsche Boerse LSE Bid. Carter Dougherty. 8 March 2005. www.nytimes.com
6. Outcome of the Berlin Summit on 22 February 2009. Press release of the German Government. 22 February 2009. www.bundesregierung. de
7. Proposal for a Directive on Alternative Investment Fund Managers. European Commission. April 2009. www.ec.europa.eu
8. Revealed: The Geithner letter to EU's Michel Barnier. Sam Jones. *Financial Times.* 11 March 2010. www.ft.com
9. Hedge Funds and Financial Crises, Strömqvist.
10. The Turner Review: A Regulatory Response to the Global Banking Crisis. Financial Services Authority. March 2009. www.fsa.gov.uk
11. High-Level Group on Financial Supervision in the EU, chaired by Jacques de Larosière. February 2009. http://ec.europa.eu
12. Rapport sur la crise financière – Mission confiée par le Président de la République dans le contexte de la Présidence française de l'Union européenne 2008. René Ricol. September 2008. www.ladocument ationfrancaise.fr
13. The Turner Review, Financial Services Authority.
14. Hedge Funds, Systemic Risk, and the Financial Crisis of 2007–2008. Written Testimony of Andrew Lo. US House of Representatives' Committee on Oversight and Government Reform. 13 November 2008. www.house.gov
15. Financial Reform – A Framework for Financial Stability. Working Group on Financial Reform. Group of Thirty. January 2009. www. group30.org
16. The Turner Review, Financial Services Authority.

31

SHORT-SELLING

The practice of short-selling stocks has also been identified as a cause of the crisis. Short-selling involves selling a financial instrument which you do not own. It subdivides into covered and naked short-selling. In the former, the seller will typically borrow the security from a holder and sell it, in the hope that s/he will be able to buy the stock back at a lower price and return it to the original owner at a profit. Naked short-selling refers to the practice of selling stocks one does not own, but without having borrowed them. In most developed markets, covered short-selling is an acceptable practice. Naked short-selling, while not normally illegal, is typically covered by a number of regulations, which may apply differentially to market makers and other participants. In recent years, the broad assumption of regulators, supported by the majority of academic research, has been that short-selling improves market liquidity and the price discovery process. While practices have varied market by market, generally short-selling has become more widely practised and subject to fewer constraints. For example, in 2007 the SEC eliminated the 'uptick rule' according to which investors could short a stock only after its price had risen, or 'ticked' higher.

Some have argued that this change, and other deregulatory moves by the SEC and authorities elsewhere, was a significant contributor to the market conditions which led to the crisis.

These arguments became much more strongly held in the autumn of 2008, where those firms which suffered very sharp falls in their stock price and, in some cases, went out of business identified short-selling as a powerful contributor to their problems. In his evidence to Congress on the failure of his firm Lehman Brothers, Dick Fuld identified naked short-selling as a powerful factor.[1] Jimmy Cayne did the same when interrogated by the Financial Crisis Inquiry Commission in May 2010. In September 2008, John Mack, then the Chairman and Chief Executive of Morgan Stanley, argued that Morgan Stanley was under attack from short-sellers also: 'it's very clear to me – we're in the midst of market control by fear and rumours and short-sellers are driving our stock down'.[2]

At the time, regulators shared that view, or at least acted as if they did. In mid-July 2008, the SEC announced emergency actions to limit the naked short-selling of Fannie Mae and Freddie Mac. That rule expired in August, but in mid-September the SEC issued new and more extensive rules against naked shorting, with the statement 'the SEC has zero tolerance for abusive naked short-selling'.[3] The FSA in London similarly outlawed short-selling in a range of financial stocks.

Most of these rules have subsequently expired. Research has shown that the percentage of all stocks affected by short-selling bans around the world rose to almost 35 per cent in November 2008, and has since fallen below 20 per cent.[4] But regulators remain concerned. The FSA has proposed additional disclosure requirements related to short positions in an attempt to enhance transparency in the market, in a way that will also have the effect of reducing the incidence of short-selling. In February 2010, the SEC approved further curbs on the practice, by a 3 to 2 vote. The Chair, Mary Schapiro, while recognizing that short-selling can benefit the market, noted 'we are concerned that excessive downwards price pressure on individual securities, accompanied by the fear of unconstrained short-selling, can destabilize our markets and undermine investor confidence'.[5]

But investigations of the circumstances surrounding the collapse of financial firms in 2008, and the market turmoil at that time, have not identified clear evidence of abusive practices. An FSA discussion paper[6] concluded that direct and permanent restrictions on short-selling in the form of a ban or an uptick rule could not be justified in normal circumstances, though it reserved the right to impose temporary bans in extreme market conditions.

Academic research, while not unanimous, has typically found that short-selling bans have adverse consequences. Beber and Pagano, reviewing short-selling bans in the crisis,[7] conclude that 'such bans can damage stock market liquidity and slow down the speed at which new information is impounded in stock prices'. Other analysts[8] find that liquidity deteriorated significantly for stocks in the US subject to the SEC ban. Beber and Pagano further maintain that 'bans on covered short sales turn out to be correlated with significantly lower excess returns relative to stocks unaffected by the ban, while bans on naked sales and disclosure obligations do not have a significant correlation with excess returns'. Furthermore, 'the bans are associated with a statistically and economically significant increase in bid-ask spreads throughout the world'. By contrast, disclosure obligations are associated with a significant decrease in bid-ask spreads. Overall, bans, as opposed to enhanced disclosure obligations, make stock prices slower to react to new information and harm price discovery, as earlier studies had shown.

That conclusion was reinforced in another paper on short-selling regulation after the financial crisis[9] which concluded that 'the available evidence on balance suggests that short-selling restrictions hamper the price discovery process', and that they are 'an ineffective detour to pursue the goal of fair markets'. Gruenewald, Wagner and Weber also hypothesize that more transparency may interfere with efficient price discovery, a finding at odds with that of Beber and Pagano. A further study by the consultancy Oliver Wyman[10] – commissioned by a hedge fund trade association – found that short-selling disclosure rules 'have materially negative impacts on market liquidity, bid-ask spreads, price discovery and intraday volatility'.

A more fundamental point made by those who do not agree with the anti-short-selling arguments is that short-selling is an inherently risky market practice. Short-sellers are vulnerable to a bear squeeze, when long holders of a stock refuse to supply them with shares, or contribute to a change in market sentiment, pushing the price up. On this analysis, short-sellers are only likely to be successful where they have identified genuine mispricing, and where a company's fortunes are deteriorating for substantive reasons. Market rumours may work in both directions, lifting stock prices as well as depressing them. And there is a puzzle about the way market participants behave. Some of those who are critical of short-selling in one context are nonetheless willing to lend their stock to facilitate the practice elsewhere.

While the crisis has provided new evidence, and in a sense acted as a case study of short-selling and its regulation, there is little sign of an emerging consensus on the practice or on the optimal regulatory environment. Those who broadly support short-selling as a legitimate market practice in most circumstances may nonetheless favour temporary bans in periods of near panic in the markets.

References

1. Testimony of Richard Fuld before the US House of Representatives – Committee on Oversight and Government Reform. 6 October 2008. http://oversight.house.gov
2. US Regulators Tighten Short-Selling Rules. Joanna Chung and Deborah Brewster. *Financial Times*. 17 September 2008. www. ft.com
3. SEC Issues New Rules to Protect Investors Against Naked Short-Selling Abuses. SEC Press Release. 17 September 2008. www.sec.gov
4. Short-Selling Bans in the Crisis: A Misguided Policy. Alessandro Beber and Marco Pagano. Vox. 6 February 2010. www.voxeu.org
5. In 3–2 Vote, SEC Limits Short Sales. *The Wall Street Journal*. 25 February 2010. www.wsj.com
6. Short-Selling. Financial Services Authority. Discussion Paper 09/1. February 2009. www.fsa.gov
7. Short-Selling Bans around the World: Evidence from the 2007–09 Crisis. Alessandro Beber and Marco Pagano. CEPR Discussion Paper No. 7557. www.cepr.org
8. Shackling the Short-Sellers: The 2008 Shorting Ban. Ekkehart Boehmer *et al.* Johnson School Research Paper Series No. 34–09. June 2009. www.johnson.cornell.edu/
9. Short-Selling Regulation after the Financial Crisis – First Principles

Revisited. Seraina Gruenewald *et al*. Swiss Finance Institute Research Paper No. 09–28. 15 December 2009. www.swissfinanceinstitute.ch/

10. The Effects of Short-Selling Public Disclosure Regimes on Equity Markets – A Comparative Analysis of US and European Markets. Bradley Ziff and Thayer Moeller. February 2010. www.oliver wyman.com

F   ECONOMICS AND FINANCE THEORY IRRATIONAL EXPECTATIONS

The belief that markets are fundamentally rational played a powerful role in forming the views of market participants and their regulators. It made the latter reluctant to challenge market and asset prices, even when they appeared inexplicable by reference to the economic fundamentals.

This belief was traced back to teaching about markets in economics departments and business schools. The 'rational expectations' underpinning of much economic analysis was identified as a particular culprit (Section 32). Similarly, the Efficient Market Hypothesis was seen as a dangerous model which influenced market behaviour in a negative way (33). The emphasis in business schools on short-term returns, and the neglect of ethical principles, have also been the subject of strong criticism (34).

32

THE DEATH OF
ECONOMICS

It was not long before the economics profession began to be identified as one of the potential culprits in the crisis blame game. Why did economists not predict the crisis? Had their work not contributed to a belief that markets and participants in them were rational, and that their self-correcting tendencies were powerful? The 'dismal science' moniker found its way into many newspaper columns. Venerable jokes about lying all the world's economists end-to-end and still not reaching a conclusion were retailed as freshly minted aphorisms. Journalists constructed vigorous arguments highlighting the profession's many weaknesses.

This was bad enough, but worse was to come. There were distinguished apostates from within the ranks who argued that academic economists did indeed have a powerful case to answer.

The most prominent internal critic was Paul Krugman. Under the title 'How Did Economists Get it So Wrong?',[1] Krugman took aim at his own profession, and particularly at the so-called Freshwater School, centred on the University of Chicago. The Freshwater School is a description used broadly to describe macroeconomists who, from the early 1970s, have shifted away from the previous consensus in macroeconomics. They base their views on a rational expectations model designed to illustrate how individuals and institutions make decisions under uncertainty. Krugman describes them as 'essentially neo-classical purists, taking their inspiration from Robert Lucas'. Saltwater economists, usually – as the name suggests – to be found in coastal US universities, 'have a more or less Keynesian vision of what recessions are all about'. In fact, Krugman's critique leaves neither school unscathed.

He acknowledges that 'few economists saw our current crisis coming, but this predictive failure was the least of the field's problems. More important was the profession's blindness to the catastrophic failures in a market economy.'[2] Referring to a 'dark age of macroeconomics',[3] he argues that the profession went astray 'because economists, as a group, mistook beauty, clad in impressive mathematics, for truth . . . this romanticized and sanitized vision of the economy led most economists to ignore all the things that can go wrong. They turned a blind eye to the limitations of human rationality that often led to bubbles and busts; to the problems of institutions that run amok; to the imperfections of markets – especially financial markets – that can cause the economy's operating systems to undergo sudden, unpredictable crashes.'[4] He was particularly critical, also, of the efficient markets hypothesis and the capital asset pricing model, as examples of the way in which this fundamentally flawed approach can lead to faulty models with damaging practical consequences.

Willem Buiter, now Chief Economist of Citigroup, developed this argument further, specifically in relation to monetary economics in a piece entitled 'The Unfortunate Uselessness of Most "State of the Art" Academic Monetary Economics'.[5] In Buiter's view, 'the typical graduate macroeconomics and monetary economics training received at Anglo-American universities during the past 30 years or so may have set back by decades serious investigations of aggregate economic behaviour and economic policy relevant understanding. It was a privately and socially costly waste of time and other resources.' Buiter himself had spent much of the past thirty years teaching in those universities, albeit with spells in the EBRD and the Bank of England. In his view, the fundamental flaw was that most economists of the freshwater and saltwater variety worked in a 'complete market paradigm', in other words in a world where there are markets for claims that cover all possible states of the world and where illiquidity is impossible. Questions about insolvency and illiquidity cannot even be asked within this framework, let alone answered. So the starting assumption dismisses many practical problems, such as those which were at the heart of the financial market crisis that played out through 2008. He sees this complete market assumption as 'the most prominent theoretical fatality'. So the models in use by many academic economists, and indeed by central banks, were of very limited use in either predicting or understanding the crisis. Dynamic stochastic general equilibrium (DSGE) models assume that, following an external shock, markets will return quickly to the deterministic steady state. These models, according to Charles Goodhart of the LSE, 'exclude everything I'm interested in', in other words everything he considers relevant to the pursuit of financial stability.

Luigi Spaventa, of the University of Rome, agrees, noting that 'DSGE models are impeccably micro-founded, but their micro-foundations are hardly compatible with credit cycles and financial dislocations . . . all very neat, but of little or no use for understanding why a financial crisis may occur and how it unfolds.'[6] The neglect of financial variables has in his view characterized a large part of modern macroeconomic modelling. As Charles Wyplosz has said, 'most macroeconomists assumed that financial markets were just a sideshow, which could safely be taken as exogenous or described in a rudimentary way'.[7] His conclusion is that economists do therefore bear some responsibility for the crisis, as their doctrines often provided intellectual justification for the unconstrained behaviour of the private sector and the negligence of regulators.

In 'The Financial Crisis and the Systemic Failure of Academic Economics', Colander et al. argue that the profession's lack of an understanding of the trends leading up to the crisis is due 'to a misallocation of research efforts in economics'.[8] Once again, the authors believe that the models in wide use disregard the key elements which drive outcomes in real world markets. Furthermore, the profession has failed to communicate the limitations, weaknesses and dangers of its preferred models, so leaving itself open to criticism when these models are misused. They argue for a major reorientation of academic economic research, particularly in the areas of behavioural and experimental economics, and network theory, which they believe have been relatively neglected. Their conclusion is that 'economics has been trapped in a suboptimal equilibrium in which much of its research efforts are not directed towards the most prevalent needs of society. Paradoxically, self-reinforcing feedback effects within the profession may have led to the dominance of a paradigm with no solid methodological basis and whose empirical performance is, to say the least, modest. Defining away the most prevalent economic problems of modern economies and failing to communicate the limitations and assumptions of its popular models, the economic profession bears some responsibility for the current crisis.'[9]

The sharpest of these criticisms have been directed at the Chicago School, seen colloquially as a hardcore sect within freshwater economists, under the intellectual leadership of Nobel prize winner Robert Lucas. Joe Stiglitz, a Nobel prize winner himself, launched the attack: 'The Chicago School bears the blame for providing a seeming intellectual foundation for the idea that markets are self-adjusting and the best role for government is to do nothing.'[10] These arguments were developed further in his 'Letter from Chicago after the Blowouts' by John Cassidy in *The New Yorker*.[11] Judge Richard Posner, who had been a leading figure in the conservative Chicago School of Economics for decades, has turned against his former colleagues. In *A Failure of Capitalism*, he criticizes Lucas and others for failing to appreciate the magnitude of the subprime crisis, and questioning the methodology that Lucas and his colleagues pioneered.[12]

The Chicago School has responded robustly to these attacks. Anna Schwartz, Milton Friedman's co-author of *A Monetary History of the United States*, is not apologetic, seeing the crisis as an isolated incident which does not invalidate the theoretical approach she takes. 'There have been business cycles for centuries, some mild, some even severe. Why should the current one be expected to alter the views of the Chicago School?'[13] Similarly, Gary Becker, another Nobel prize winner, defended the principles which have guided freshwater economics for decades. 'I don't think any of the major ideas were wrong. If you look at the role of markets and competition in promoting economic growth over the last 25 years, things look very well, even if you factor in this serious recession'.[14] Fellow Nobel prize winner, Heckman, completely rejects the idea that economists are to blame for the crisis, arguing that the collapse was caused by government regulators and Wall Street traders ignoring Chicago principles. 'We should really ask who were the people in 2000 who decided that markets don't need regulating. Those were not Chicago economists. Some of them were Clinton officials, and some of them are now advising Obama.'[15] Lucas himself has rejected the caricature of economists educated in the use of valueless, even harmful, mathematical models as 'nonsense'. He maintains that the efficient market hypothesis remains broadly robust and that we will never find models that forecast sudden falls in the values of financial assets such as those which followed the failure of Lehman Brothers. Until the Lehman failure, 'the recession was pretty typical of the modest downturns of the post-War period'. So, in his view, the deep recession of 2008–2009 was a failure of policy making and not of economic analysis.[16] He maintains that mainstream economic thinking has developed many useful theoretical models. 'I simply see no connection between the reality of macroeconomics . . . and the caricature provided by the critics.'

These sharply contrasting views seem to admit little prospect of accommodation. But Barry Eichengreen of the University of California at Berkeley attempts to find a 'third way' which acknowledges the force of some of the criticisms of the profession, but without accepting the degree of culpability which they imply. He argues that it was not that economic theory had nothing to say 'about those kinds of structural weaknesses and conflicts of interest that paved the way to our current catastrophe. In fact, large swaths of modern economic theory focus squarely on the kind of economic problems that created our current mess. The problem was not an inability to imagine that conflicts of interest, self-dealing and herd behaviour could arise, but a peculiar failure to apply those insights to the real world.'[17] He notes the relevance of agency theory and inflation economics to financial market malfunctions, and also to the work done on moral hazard by many economists. He points to the behavioural economics work which explains how emotion and psychological and social factors affect decision making.

He praises the work of George Akerlof and Robert Schiller in understanding real-life market behaviour. He therefore maintains that it was not 'the limits of scholarly imagination' that created the problem, but 'the problem was a partial and blinkered reading of the literature. The consumers of economic theory, not surprisingly, tended to pick and choose those elements of that rich literature that best supported their self-serving actions. Equally reprehensibly, the producers of that theory, benefitting in ways both pecuniary and psychic, showed disturbingly little tendency to reject. It is in this light that we must understand how it was that the vast majority of the economics profession remained so blissfully silent and indeed unaware of the risk of financial disaster.'

Economists, he argues, were often too close to financial market participants and ready to accept consultancy assignments and well-paid speaking engagements from financial firms. As a result, they were subject to a form of 'cognitive regulatory capture'. Scholars, in his view, are no more immune than regulators to this syndrome.

Eichengreen's conclusion is, however, broadly optimistic. He acknowledges the risk that economists will remain doomed to repeat past mistakes, but identifies a reason for hope amidst the gloom. He considers that the last decade has seen a quiet revolution in the practice of economics, with much greater value now given to empirical work than was the case even in the quite recent past. He sees the late twentieth century as 'the hey-day of deductive economics. Talented and facile purists set the intellectual agenda.' But, by contrast, he believes, or perhaps hopes, that 'the 21st century will be the age of inductive economists when empiricists hold sway and advice is grounded in concrete observation of markets and their inhabitants'.

Can we identify support to buttress this optimistic prognosis? Certainly, in economics departments on both sides of the Atlantic, there are signs of retrospection and self-criticism. At the LSE, Tim Besley says 'we need to try to bring in some of the insights of psychology . . . [and] . . . to respect the role of institutional arrangements – the ways in which different structures shape the way the economy works'. In relation to the role of markets 'we introduce the market model and then we introduce a wide range of caveats as to why the market may not perform as the textbook says . . . more of the caveats should be part of the core'.[18] George Soros has committed $50 million to support an 'Institute of New Economic Thinking', whose aim is to encourage an overhaul of economic teaching and research. The Institute was launched at a conference in Cambridge in April 2010.

The profession has been stung by the attacks on it, especially those of the critics within its ranks. But it is too early to say whether this self-critical mood will result in a change in the profession's intellectual centre of gravity and in undergraduate and graduate curricula.

References

1. How Did Economists Get It So Wrong? Paul Krugman. *The New York Times*. 6 September 2009. www.nytimes.com
2. A Dark Age of Macroeconomics. Paul Krugman. 27 January 2009. http://krugman.blogs.nytimes.com
3. Ibid.
4. How Did Economists Get It So Wrong?, Krugman.
5. The Unfortunate Uselessness of Most 'State of the Art' Academic Monetary Economics. Willem Buiter. 3 March 2009. http://blogs.ft.com/maverecon
6. Economists and Economics: What Does the Crisis Tell Us? Luigi Spaventa. Centre for Economic Policy Research. Policy Insight No. 38. August 2009. www.cepr.org
7. Macroeconomics After the Crisis: Dealing with the Tobin curse. Charles Wyplosz. Walter-Adolf-Joehr Lecture. 15 May 2009.
8. The Financial Crisis and the Systemic Failure of Academic Economics. David Colander *et al*. Kiel Institute For the World Economy No. 1489. February 2009.
9. Ibid.
10. Ibid.
11. Letter from Chicago: After the Blowup. John Cassidy. *The New Yorker*. 11 January 2010. http://www.newyorker.com/
12. *A Failure of Capitalism*. Richard A. Posner. Harvard University Press. 2009.
13. Chicago Schooled. Michael Fitzgerald. The University Of Chicago Magazine. October 2009. http://magazine.uchicago.edu
14. Ibid.
15. Ibid.

16. In Defence of the Dismal Science. Robert Lucas. *The Economist*. 6 August 2009.
17. The Last Temptation of Risk. Barry Eichengreen. The National Interest. May/June 2009.
18. Time for State Control and Free Market Economics to Come Together. Roman Chlupatý. *Czech Business Weekly*. 9 March 2010. www.cbw.cz

33

INEFFICIENT MARKETS

The links between economic theory and financial market theory are close. But there are some specific criticisms of financial market theory which complement those of economics and, in some ways, extend them. They focus particularly on the efficient market hypothesis (EMH), and the capital asset pricing model (CAPM). The efficient market hypothesis, most associated with Professor Eugene Fama at the University of Chicago, asserts that financial markets are informationally efficient, in that prices on traded assets reflect all publicly available information. There are stronger versions of the hypothesis which maintain that prices also instantly change to reflect the arrival of new public information, or even that they incorporate information not publicly available.

The CAPM asserts that the market prices of individual securities are fairly determined, using a risk-reward ratio for any particular asset in relation to the risks in the overall market. Each security is ascribed a beta, reflecting its risk relative to the market as a whole. The CAPM holds that investors are not rewarded for undiversified risk in their portfolios, but only for systematic risk. This beguiling theory, in spite of the many weaknesses which have been exposed in recent decades, remains at the heart of much research and teaching about the behaviour of capital markets.

The remarkable behaviour of asset prices during the crisis

has prompted renewed criticism, and some have gone so far as to argue that the models themselves were in large part responsible for the behaviour which led first to the boom, and then to the bust. They caused politicians, central bankers and regulators to place excessive reliance on market rationality, which caused them to fail to intervene to prick the bubble.

A prominent critic is Jeremy Grantham, the Principal of GMO, a large institutional asset management company in Boston, with a strong record of performance. Grantham wrote, 'in their desire for mathematical order and elegant models, the economic establishment played down the role of bad behaviour . . . and flat-out bursts of irrationality'.[1] He continued, 'the incredibly inaccurate efficient market theory was believed in totality by many of our financial leaders . . . it left our economic and governmental establishment sitting by confidently, even as a lethally dangerous combination of asset bubbles, lax controls, pernicious incentives and wickedly complicated instruments led to our plight.'[2]

Justin Fox, a business columnist for *Time* magazine, in 'The Myth of the Rational Market', charts the rise and fall of the efficient market hypothesis.[3] Hans Blommestein, a Professor of Finance at Tillburg University in the Netherlands, advances a more academic, but no less damning critique: 'Most research programmes in academic finance . . . have systematically neglected the implications of the nature and limitations of economics as a social science . . . this has had adverse, perhaps even fatal, consequences for the use or interpretation of these models . . . by practitioners.'[4] He relates the weaknesses of the models specifically to the structured products such as CDOs and CDSs, whose behaviour was at the core of the problem. The pricing of risk in those instruments is, he argues, 'based on the key theoretical notion of perfect replication. Naturally, perfect replication does not exist in reality and has to be approximated . . . instead, researchers and practitioners had to rely on simulation based pricing machines.' These mechanisms 'constitute an unsound scientific basis for the reliable pricing of risk'. He believes that academics should have been outspoken in criticizing the use of these models which led to artificial pricing and, indirectly, to bubbles.

Blommestein goes on to maintain that these theoretical

constructs, with their inbuilt errors, were at the heart of the financial models used by financial firms themselves to understand the risks they ran. These models are, therefore, fundamentally flawed. 'Typically, value at risk models do not take into account the fact that development in financial markets will induce similar and simultaneous behaviour by numerous players; in other words, strategic factors in the behaviour of market participants are neglected.'[5]

Robert Schiller has demonstrated that financial market prices can diverge significantly, and for a long period, from the prices indicated by the models or by economic analysis. He borrows a Greenspan phrase to characterize this as attributable to 'Irrational Exuberance'.[6]

George Soros has developed a similar line of argument. He believes that market prices are influenced by feedback loops. He disputes the basis of equilibrium theory, in which prices in the long run at equilibrium reflect the underlying fundamentals, which are themselves unaffected by prices. The theory of reflexivity, as advanced by Soros, asserts that prices do in fact influence the fundamentals which in turn change expectations, thus once again influencing those prices. Eventually, this feedback loop turns on itself, generating the collapse to follow the bubble. He argues that the bubble which preceded the crisis was influenced by 'the prevailing misconception . . . that financial markets are self-correcting and should be left to their own devices'.[7] This, however, is not the only form of reflexivity. The inflation and subsequent deflation of bubbles 'are only the most dramatic and the most directly opposed to the efficient market hypothesis . . . but reflexivity can take many other forms. In currency markets, the upside and downside are symmetrical . . . but there is no sign of equilibrium either. Floating exchange rates tend to move in large, multi-year waves.'[8]

In his review of the crisis, Adair Turner asserted the following: 'at the core of these assumptions [leading to the crisis] has been the theory of efficient and rational markets. Five propositions with implications for regulatory approach have followed:

(1) Market prices are a good indicator of rationally evaluated economic value.
(2) The development of securitized credit, since based on the

creation of new and more liquid markets, has improved by allocative efficiency of financial markets.

(3) The risk characteristics of financial markets can be inferred from mathematical analysis, delivering robust quantitative measures of trading risk.

(4) Market discipline can be used as an effective tool in constraining harmful risk-taking.

(5) Financial innovation can be assumed to be beneficial since market competition would eliminate any innovations which did not deliver value added.

Each of these assumptions is now subject to extensive challenge on both theoretical and empirical grounds, with potential implications for the appropriate design of regulation and for the role of regulatory authorities.'[9]

But these critics of the EMH have provoked strong responses from defenders of the theory. They accept that the strong form version is not unambiguously supported by market experience, and acknowledge that the crisis is in the nature of a 'black swan'. But they reject the view that it is attributable to blind acceptance of the EMH. Fama has argued that the proposition that the hypothesis lies behind the crisis is 'fantasy'. 'Most investing is done by active managers who don't believe markets are efficient . . . about 80 per cent of mutual fund wealth is actively managed. Hedge funds, private equity and other alternative asset classes . . . are built on the proposition that markets are inefficient.' He rejects the popular story that financial markets caused the recession: 'I think one can take an entirely different position: financial markets and financial institutions were casualties rather than the cause of the recession.' In his view, the growth of finance has played a big role in the rapid growth of the world economy over the last twenty years and, in spite of the booms and busts, 'provides a good view of the world for almost all practical purposes'.[10]

Economists also point out that the quantitative models used in banks and rating agencies for risk management and valuation are more often than not the product of mathematicians and scientists with very little knowledge of economics.

Ray Ball, of the University of Chicago's Booth School of Business, has contested the critics' detailed arguments, especially those put forward by Turner. He disputes the idea that the EMH was a decisive influence on regulatory behaviour. 'If regulators had been true believers in efficiency, they would have been considerably more sceptical about some of the consistently high returns being reported by various financial institutions. If the capital market is fiercely competitive, there is a good chance that high returns are attributable to high leverage, high risk, inside information or dishonest accounting. True believers in efficiency would have looked more closely at the leverage and risk-taking positions of Lehman Brothers . . . and investment banks generally.'

He accepts that the efficient markets hypothesis is a theory, and no more, and that it does not explain every behaviour in financial markets. Furthermore, there are limitations, particularly, 'the theory makes no statements whatsoever about the supply side of the information market: about how much information is available'. The CAPM is vulnerable to criticism, too, on the basis that it takes the riskless rate, the market risk premium and individual security beaters as given, while in the event of a large market shock the values of these parameters are highly uncertain. So it is clear that the EMH adopts a simplified view of markets. He acknowledges that behavioural finance 'has succeeded in poking many more holes in the theory of efficient markets' but that 'taken as a whole, [it] consists of a set of disjointed and inconsistent ideas, some of which are rationalizations of the anomalies of others' and therefore does not amount to a rival set of theories. In his view, therefore, 'the theory of efficient markets is appearing to be durable, and seems likely to continue to be so despite its inevitable and painfully obvious limitations'.[11]

Similarly, many economists and financial market theorists have been robust in their criticism of George Soros' theories of reflexivity, on the grounds that while they may have some descriptive force in relation to observed behaviours in markets, they do not amount to a usable theory which can explain market behaviour in the longer term. Some defenders of the EMH argue that the crisis better illustrates the failure of the theory of incomplete and imperfect markets. But the crisis has undoubtedly weakened the underpinnings of modern academic finance theory, and the process of constructing a revised theoretical architecture is under way. At the LSE, for example, the Paul Woolley Centre of the Study of Capital Market Dysfunctionality (established just before the crisis) has begun to publish a series of papers designed to understand better the dynamics of modern markets.[12] There are other initiatives elsewhere, but a comprehensive new theory, with the simplicity and apparent explanatory power of the EMH, may be some while away.

References

1. Obama and the Teflon Men, and Other Short Stories. Jeremy Grantham. GMO Quarterly Letter. January 2009. www.gmo.com
2. Ibid.
3. The Myth of the Rational Market. Justin Fox. HarperBusiness. New York 2009.
4. The Financial Crisis as a Symbol of the Failure of Academic Finance? Hans Blommestein. *Journal of Financial Transformation* 2009, Vol. 27.
5. Ibid.
6. *Irrational Exuberance*. Robert Schiller. Princeton University Press. 2000.
7. Financial Markets. George Soros. Lecture at the Central European University. 27 October 2009.
8. The Turner Review: A Regulatory Response to the Global Banking Crisis. Financial Services Authority. March 2009. www.fsa.gov.uk
9. Ibid.
10. Is Market Efficiency the Culprit? Eugene Fama. Fama/French Forum. 4 November 2009. www.dimensional.com
11. The Global Financial Crisis and the Efficient Market Hypothesis. Ray Ball. *Journal of Applied Corporate Finance* Fall 2009, Vol. 21, No. 4.
12. The Paul Woolley Working Papers Series include: An Institutional Theory of Momentum and Reversal. Dimitri Vayanos, Paul Woolley. November 2008; Liquidity and Asset Prices: A United Framework. Dimitri Vayanos, Jiang Wang. July 2009. www.lse.ac.uk/collections/paulWoolleyCentre/

34

AN ETHICS-FREE ZONE BUSINESS SCHOOLS

Beyond the specific criticism of the financial models and financial theories used in banks and securities firms (Section 33), there is a broader critique of the pernicious influence of business school education, especially, but not exclusively, in the United States.

While only around one third of corporate Chief Executives in the US have MBA degrees,[1] many of the Wall Street titans associated with the high profile collapses were trained at top ranked business schools. Dick Fuld of Lehman Brothers is a graduate of NYU Stern School of Business, and Stan O'Neal and his successor John Thain are both Harvard MBAs.

There is Stanford research[2] that the impact of business schools on American corporations may be less marked than many think. Jeffrey Pfeffer quotes evidence showing that firms led by CEOs without MBAs had 'slightly better risk adjusted market performance'. But the argument advanced by the financial crisis critics is that business schools had a decisive influence on corporate culture which, in turn, led to the excesses whose high price we are now paying.

Jay Lorsch and Rakesh Khurana of Harvard Business School maintain that 'models of corporate leadership that value leaders' charisma over substance, an uncritical embrace of laissez-faire models – were taught to MBA and executive students without considering whether these ideas and tools would contribute to a firm's long-term wellbeing or would endanger the legitimacy of the US capital system.'[3] In a *Harvard Business Review* online poll, respondents sympathized with this line of attack. Two out of three respondents maintained that business schools were at least partially responsible for their graduates' ethical lapses.[4] Other business school leaders support a similar line. Angel Cabrera, the President of Thunderbird School of Global Management, says that 'MBAs create a dominant view of business and its language and tools. To say that we have no responsibility is to say the MBA is irrelevant.'[5]

Similar arguments have been advanced in the UK. While the MBA qualification is less ubiquitous on the eastern side of the Atlantic, some of the principal architects of the crash were business school graduates. Andy Hornby, the then Chief Executive of Halifax Bank of Scotland, and a Harvard MBA, is an example. The losses at HBOS were dramatically large: lending standards were astonishingly low. Under the headline 'Academies of the Apocalypse', *The Guardian* argued that business schools 'flooded the banking world with graduates of their prestigious MBA courses. They then helped the economy to nosedive.'[6] A particular criticism on the European side is that there has been a failure to incorporate corporate social responsibility and business ethics firmly into courses. According to the Association of MBAs, just 20 per cent of UK MBA courses have a mandatory CSR module.[7]

That ethical gap seems to be reflected in business behaviour. A study by three academics at Rutgers, Washington State and Penn State noted that MBA students are more likely to cheat than others. 56 per cent of MBA students admitted that they cheat in class, versus 47 per cent of non-business students.[8]

Those who support this line of argument see business schools at a turning point. Jay Light, the Dean of Harvard Business School, has said, 'we've had a spectacular 25 year period of primarily growth, primarily profits. We've spent less and less time thinking about the other side: what could go wrong. And that, for sure, I think we should have all been thinking more about. I think business schools are included.'[9] At Harvard and elsewhere, task forces have been established to try and identify how well schools prepared students before the financial crisis, and to highlight changes that are needed.

Cabrera argues that management needs to be calm, for 'it's a true profession' with its own code of conduct to parallel those in medicine and law. 'I have no doubt that if we had been successful at creating a consensus around a set of principles across business schools around the world, decisions would have been quite different.'

But there is no consensus, either within or outside business schools, on this point. Others argue that it is quite wrong to blame business schools, rather than the firms who hired their graduates. Andrew Lo of the Sloan School of Management at MIT argues that 'by training tomorrow's leaders to manage the risks of the financial system effectively and ethically, we'll have a fighting chance of surviving even the largest crisis. This is what business schools do, and we need more of it, not less.'[10] Others maintain that the crisis in fact validates much business school education. Anant Sundaram of the Tuck School of Business says, 'what we witnessed in the capital markets violates Finance 101 ideas'.[11] He says that 'once business school graduates get sucked into the murky world of Wall Street, where risk and reward are divorced',[12] they begin to behave in ways which are quite different from those which they have been taught. On this analysis, perhaps the worst that can be said of business schools is that their education and analytics are not sufficiently robust to arm graduates with the defences which allow them to resist temptation and irrational exuberance.

References

1. Leadership Development in Business Schools: An Agenda for Change. Jeffrey Pfeffer. Stanford University Graduate School of Business Research Paper No. 2016. 14 February 2009.
2. Ibid.
3. Financial Crisis: Blame B-schools. Jay Lorsch, Rakesh Khurana, Andrew Lo. BusinessWeek Debate Room. November 2008. www.businessweek.com
4. Are Business Schools to Blame for the Crisis? TraderMark. SeekingAlpha. 26 May 2009. http://seekingalpha.com
5. Ibid.

6. Academies of the Apocalypse? Adam James. *The Guardian*. 7 April 2009. www.guardian.co.uk

7. Ibid.

8. Academic Dishonesty in Graduate Business Programs: Prevalence, Causes, and Proposed Action. Donald McCabe *et al*. *Academy of Management Learning & Education* 2006, Vol. 5, No. 3.

9. Business Schools Mull Over Blame in Financial Crisis. Anthony Brooks. 17 May 2009. www.npr.org

10. Financial Crisis, Lorsch *et al*.

11. Are B-schools to Blame? David Serchuk. 4 May 2009. www.forbes.com

12. Ibid.

G   WILD CARDS

The blame game has extended beyond the financial sector, and outside the confines of monetary policy and regulation.

Why did the fearless media not raise the alarm? Were journalists, too, caught up in the general euphoria, and the reverence for wealth (Section 35)?

Are there societal or physiological explanations for behaviours in financial firms which now seem, at best, bizarre. Perhaps greed, normally moderated by fear of loss, got the upper hand in a long period in which it was very easy to make money (36). Did video games contribute to a sense of distance between real world events and the screens in trading rooms (37)? Was there a hormonal explanation for excessive risk-taking in securities firms, especially by young men (38)?

35

THE WATCHDOG THAT DIDN'T BARK THE MEDIA

In retrospect, some of the trends which led to the explosion of 2007–08 look so extreme that it is hard to understand how they could have been so widely ignored by the commentators and the broader public. Why did the business and financial press not see the problem coming? The press, unlike the regulators, has no statutory responsibility to guard against financial excess, but were there no sceptics who questioned the sustainability of the dramatic growth in credit and asset prices that was under way? Some politicians, on both sides of the Atlantic, have been vociferous in arguing that the media fell down on its job, just as central banks and regulators did. In London, a parliamentary committee summoned representatives of the press to discuss their role, and criticized them both for failing to alert the country to the emerging crisis, and for making it worse through alarmist reporting.[1] These criticisms generated predictably enraged responses from the media itself, together with some selective quotations from past articles which drew attention to subsets of the problem.

The *Columbia Journalism Review* in New York has attempted to bring analysis to bear on this issue. The title of the resulting article 'Power Problem: The Business Press did Everything but Take on the Institutions that Brought Down the Financial System'[2] summarizes their conclusions. The project they undertook had one objective, 'to assess whether the business press, as it claims, provided the public with fair warnings of looming dangers during the years when it could have made a difference'. The conclusion was that 'the answer is no . . . this is the watchdog that didn't bark'.

They analysed 730 articles published between 1 January 2000 and 30 June 2007, from publications in the US (largely) but also the UK – the *Financial Times*. They asked the news outlets to volunteer their best work. Their assessment suggests that there was some useful analytical work done between 2000 and 2003, particularly focused on the lower end of the mortgage market, when subprime lending was beginning to expand. There were some revealing exposés of practices among subprime lenders, including those which collapsed so comprehensively in 2007. Some practical consequences arose from these exposés, including prohibitions on predatory lending in a number of states. But they conclude that 'any fair reading of the record will show that the business press simply lost its taste for predatory lending investigations and developed a case of collective amnesia about Wall Street's connection to subprime, rediscovering it only after the fact'. Many articles lavished praise on firms and individuals who were subsequently identified for having been most responsible for excess and bad management. For example, *The New York Times* in 2003 praised Jimmy Cayne under the headline: 'Distinct Culture at Bear Stearns Helps It Surmount a Grim Market'[3] and *Fortune* identified Stan O'Neal of Merrill Lynch as 'the most ruthless CEO in America. Merrill Lynch couldn't be luckier to have him.'[4] They conclude 'the business press institutionally lost whatever taste it had for head-on investigations of core practices of powerful institutions'.[5]

Others have supported this assessment. Daniel Schechter argues that the media failed in two key areas. There was little or no investigation of the new breed of exotic financial products, such as CDOs, and it also ignored the warnings from community housing organizations of the predatory lending practices in some of America's poorest communities.[6]

Why might this failure have occurred? How was it that the media failed to bark? A number of possible explanations have been advanced:

(1) Journalists are as influenced as anyone else by collective euphoria. J.K. Galbraith argued that journalists and others who speak out publicly against financial euphoria 'will be the exception to a very broad and binding rule. They will be required to resist two compelling forces: one, the powerful personal interest that develops in the euphoric belief, and the other, the pressure of the public and seemingly superior financial opinion that is brought to bear on such financial belief.'[7]

(2) The influence of financial public relations on the media has grown. An LSE study[8] identifies that the sums spent on financial PR rose over six times in the UK in a decade. So, as one British journalist confessed, 'if you really want to know what is going on in business in the City, don't bother reading the financial press. 90 per cent of their stories have come hot off the fax machines of public relations firms, or have been "provided" by one of the innumerable PR men who stalk the Square Mile.'[9]

(3) While the public relations industry grew, the resources of newsrooms contracted, as the business models of traditional media have been challenged by the growth of new media which has reduced sales and advertising revenue. Many newspapers cannot afford to employ relatively expensive business and financial journalists (though as the Columbia study points out, during the relevant period *Bloomberg News* employed 2,300 business journalists and *The Wall Street Journal* more than 700).

(4) Links between the media and financial firms themselves have become uncomfortably close. Since journalists rely heavily on sources in companies for their data, they develop an interest in pleasing those sources. So, 'access to information is granted; but only on condition that stories are presented in the required manner.'[10]

(5) There is a failure of understanding. Both Robert Peston of the BBC and Gillian Tett of the *Financial Times*, two journalists with a good record during the crisis if not necessarily before it, have argued that journalists found it extremely difficult to understand the nature of the new products being traded, and often therefore focused on the wrong things. So too much media reporting concentrates on the

equity markets, while the emerging problems were in the debt and derivatives markets, which are far harder to explain to the public.

(6) The media are vulnerable, as are other people, to a version of 'hero worship'. So much reporting has been personalized, with a tendency to exaggerate the skills, prescience and moral rectitude of the heroes running large financial firms. There was an exaggerated reverence for great wealth. If people are paid so much, surely they must be doing something very right?

(7) There is also the influence of advertisers. Schechter maintains that 'there is a connection between the real estate and newspaper industries . . . the newspaper industry is the marketing arm of the real estate industry'.[11] That connection was of particular significance in a crisis which began in the subprime mortgage sector.

All of these factors may have come together to create what LSE researchers have called 'a crisis for financial journalism'. The Director of the LSE Centre for the study of journalism and society, Polis, concludes, 'I cannot name a single journalist or economist who actually predicted what has happened in its totality.'[12] And there is some evidence that journalists themselves are unhappy about the performance of their profession. A survey of 100 journalists in the United States showed that sixty-two of them 'criticize the media's work, suggesting there was an overexuberance about the economy and a failure to connect the dots as troubles began.'[13]

There are counter arguments. In the *American Journalism Review*, Chris Roush[14] lists several articles which did warn about some aspects of the mortgage markets and derivatives. Sarah Bartlett, of the City University of New York's graduate school of Journalism, says, 'I take umbrage at the notion that financial journalists have let us down, it's just not true.'[15] Bartlett is a former journalist of *Business Week* and *The New York Times*. She and others say government regulators and the general public were not paying attention to the warnings which appeared in the press. And she argues that the climate was simply hostile to sceptical journalism. 'The culture encouraged people to minimize risk. Nobody wanted to think about risk.'[16] On this argument, while the press could offer critical commentary from time to time, the culture of the moment prevented that commentary from being heard and understood.

References

1. Oral Evidence N. 197 – Banking Crisis Inquiry. Treasury Committee. 4 February 2009. www.publications.parliament.uk/
2. Power Problem: The Business Press did Everything but Take on the Institutions that Brought Down the Financial System. Dean Starkman. *Columbia Journalism Review*. 1 May 2009.
3. Distinct Culture at Bear Stearns Helps It Surmount a Grim Market. Landon Thomas. *The New York Times*. 28 March 2003. www.nytimes.com
4. Putting The Muscle Back In The Bull. David Rynecki. Fortune. 5 April 2004. http://money.cnn.com/
5. Power Problem, Starkman.
6. Financial Crisis: A Media Failure? Katherine Thompson. The Editors Weblog. November 2008. www.editorsweblog.org
7. *A Short History of Financial Euphoria*. John Kenneth Galbraith. Penguin Business. London 1990, as quoted in reference below.
8. What is Financial Journalism For? Ethics and Responsibility in a Time of Crisis and Change. Damian Tambini. POLIS, LSE. November 2008. www.polismedia.org/
9. Ibid.
10. The Media and Asset Prices. Alexander Dyck and Luigi Zingales. Unpublished Working Paper, 2003, as quoted in reference above.
11. Financial Crisis: A Media Failure?, Thompson.
12. What is Financial Journalism For?, Tambini.
13. Abrams Research Survey: Financial Journalists Say Media Dropped Ball on Crisis. David Bauder. *The Huffington Post*. 8 January 2009. www.huffingtonpost.com
14. Unheeded Warnings. Chris Roush. *American Journalism Review*. December/January 2009.
15. Ibid.
16. Ibid.

36

GREED IS BAD

There are few repeatable jokes about the crisis. Dr Rowan Williams, the Archbishop of Canterbury, essayed one: when asked in October 2008 who was most responsible for the credit crunch, he replied 'I was going to suggest Satan', but added 'clearly as religious leaders we want to say that the root of it is human greed'.[1] He was presenting a report from a conference of Christian and Muslim leaders which reflected on the crisis from the perspective of Islam, which prohibits charging interest on loans, and Christianity, which does not impose such a prohibition, but which teaches against financial exploitation of the weak and vulnerable. The same argument was presented subsequently by the Dalai Lama who, in answering a question about the underlying cause of the economic crisis, said, 'too much speculation and ultimately greed'.[2]

Another proponent of the greed hypothesis is Prime Minister Kevin Rudd of Australia, who said 'if you want a definition of social injustice, this was it in brutal colour – millions of innocent workers losing their jobs because a few thousand financial executives around the world surrendered any pretence of social responsibility in their blind pursuit of absolute greed'.[3] He was speaking to an audience at the Brotherhood of St Laurence in Melbourne.

But what exactly is meant by this condemnation of greed, and identification of it as the driving force behind the collapse in financial markets in 2007? Some of the arguments advanced seem to fall straightforwardly into the category of political rhetoric. Advocates of this line of reasoning typically disagree fundamentally with the underpinnings of Western financial markets. So, for example, a Christian website, Ekklesia, argues that 'this financial crisis is a major spiritual crisis. It is a crisis of a society that worships at the temples of consumption and . . . that idealizes money above love, community, well-being and the sustainability of our planet. And it is a crisis . . . for faith organizations that have colluded . . . by tolerating the sin of usury.'[4] Some Muslim commentators have espoused the same argument. This line of attack permits no accommodation with financial markets or the principles of the Western economy.

Others, however, do not take such a fundamentalist view, and advance a more nuanced argument. Simon Longstaff, Executive Director of St James Ethics Centre, pointed to a failure of ethics and 'a failure to properly understand the kind of obligations that attach to various organs within the market system'.[5] The opportunities for short-term financial gain perverted the normal principles of doing business which guide most market participants, most of the time. The Gordon Gekko 'greed is good' factor overrode the usual principles of deferred consumption and prudence. As Larry Zicklin, a professor of business ethics at New York University's Stern School, argued, 'greed overcame due diligence'.[6] Psychologists often define self-control as the ability to negotiate a situation in which there are two choices and one is obviously superior, but the other choice is nonetheless tempting. It would appear that in this sense lenders failed to exercise self-control when they agreed to write imprudent mortgages in order to bank short-term profits. On the other side of that transaction, borrowers took on debt well beyond what they could realistically expect to repay. The desire to consume housing, or indeed other things financed by equity release from housing, overcame the principle of self-control. That is perhaps a less value-laden description of the mechanism of greed.

But why should what is a permanent feature of human motivation have produced such dramatic consequences? Greed, after all, is always with us. Defined as 'excess desire to acquire or possess more (especially material wealth) than one needs or deserves', it is 'simply the compulsion that helps anthropomorphise the capitalistic spirit. There is nothing necessarily right or wrong with greed, and there is no magical measuring stick to measure when an escalation of greed goes from being a good thing to bad. Rather, there is only greed – something that in and of itself does not cause financial crises, and something that does not drive people.'[7] It would seem, therefore, that some other factors must come into play. One man's greed is another's desire to improve his standard of living and that of his family. Without that motivation, the world would be a poorer place.

Neuroeconomists have attempted an answer. They argue[8] that in financial markets, in normal circumstances, greed and fear are balancing forces, with corresponding balancing emotional forces in the human brain, known as homeostasis. But in the crisis, the homeostasis of the reward/loss symptom of the individuals involved was thrown out of balance: 'all perception of risk was removed and therefore untrammelled greed took over in investors' brains . . . this greed stimulated a moral meltdown in the financial marketplace – a quest for money above all else'.

It is true that some people became incontinently rich during the period leading up to the crash. The spread of incomes and wealth widened in the United States and elsewhere. The 'returns to greed' grew sharply during this period, perhaps offering such dramatic returns to short-run rent-seeking behaviour as to distort individuals' priorities. The greed argument, therefore, while it seems inadequate as a self-standing explanation, cannot be easily dismissed as a contributory factor. But the surrounding conditions must have altered in a significant way, to turn a potentially dynamic factor in the economy into a destructive force.

References

1. Rowan Williams Says 'Human Greed' to Blame for Financial Crisis. Ruth Gledhill. Times Online. 15 October 2008. www.timesonline. co.uk

2. The Dalai Lama Blames 'Greed' for Financial Crisis. Tejinder Singh. NewEurope. 8 December 2008. www.neurope.eu/
3. Greed Caused Financial Crisis, Rudd Says. ABC News. 16 October 2009. www.abc.net.au
4. Economic Greed is a Spiritual Crisis. Ann Pettifor. Ekklesia. 12 October 2008. www.ekklesia.co.uk/
5. Financial Crisis is Not Just About Greed, says Ethicist. ABC News. 11 April 2009.
6. 'A Race to the Bottom': Assigning Responsibility for the Financial Crisis. Universia Knowledge @ Wharton. www.wharton.universia.net accessed 16 February 2010.
7. Financial Crisis Blaming the Culture of Greed? Brady Willett. The Market Oracle. 7 April 2009. www.marketoracle.co.uk
8. The Global Financial Crisis – Caused by Greed, Moral Meltdown and Public Policy Disasters. Donald Wargo *et al*. Report to the Forum on Public Policy: A Journal of the Oxford Round Table. March 2009. www.thefreelibrary.com

37

LARA CROFT
VIDEO GAMES

An alternative hypothesis as to why bankers might have become more reckless has been advanced by Susan Greenfield, a professor of Synaptic Pharmacology at Oxford. She asks, 'what if the recent wave of recklessness among bankers was due, in part, to the fact that the younger generation has been brought up in two dimensions – subjected to long times in front of a screen, immersed in a world of computer games?'. She posits that 'reckless behaviour is related to a mindset where the prefrontal cortex under-functions and a premium consequently shifts to the excitement and thrill of the here and now. Second, our brains are shaped by the environment. Third, if the screen culture creates a world dominated by sensation and process, rather than by content, significance and narrative, it may well be that those playing computer games have brains that adjust appropriately.'[1]

In other words, watching video games contributes to an under-functioning of the prefrontal cortex and therefore a switch away from normal adult preoccupations with the past and the future, and the consequences of one's actions. Also, the world of games, where you proceed from level to level annihilating galaxies of hostile creatures, is one 'where you can always play the game again, where there are no irreversible consequences'. That mindset carries over onto the trading floor. Traders aggressively bet against competitors, using money from shareholders (or even possibly from taxpayers) with the mindset which tells them that this is all 'only a game'.

This hypothesis is untested. Greenfield has applied for a grant to assess it. She has attracted much criticism from other scientists who question every link in the chain of argument.[2] It has been described as 'speculative flimflam, dressed up in a science-y gloss'. How does this explain the behaviour of the senior leaders of the institutions, who were certainly not brought up on video games? How do we explain previous crises, from tulips to dot-coms? Was not the behaviour of many of these traders entirely rational, given the rewards they could earn in the short term, leaving no need for an exotic 'tomb raider' explanation? So the thesis fails to present good evidence 'that the behaviour exhibited in the run-up to the credit crunch was particularly reckless or irrational . . . or that . . . it was caused by computer games rather than other social factors'.[3] We do not, therefore, seem yet to have enough evidence to indict Lara Croft.

References

1. Did Video Games Make Bankers More Reckless? Susan Greenfield. *Wired Magazine*. 27 May 2009. www.wired.co.uk
2. Speculation, Hypothesis and Ideas: But Where's the Evidence? Ben Goldacre. *The Guardian*. 15 May 2009. http://guardian.co.uk
3. Susan Greenfield on Bankers and Computer Games: Badly Thought-Out Hypothesising. Patrick Holford. Holford Watch. 11 May 2009. http://holfordwatch.info

38

HORMONES

Psychologists and behaviouralists have sought to identify the underlying personal characteristics which might lead to exaggerated risk-seeking behaviour. Researchers have also looked for physiological differences which might illuminate these phenomena.

The trading rooms of investment banks, brokers and hedge funds are male-dominated environments. Attention is therefore focused on the question of the extent to which masculine characteristics are associated with risky behaviours. An article in *Scientific American*[1] asked bluntly 'is testosterone to blame for the financial crisis?'. It referenced a Harvard study which took saliva samples from a hundred male students before they played an investment game with real money. The researchers found that 'risk-taking in an investment game with potential for real monetary payoffs correlates positively with salivary testosterone levels and facial masculinity, with the latter being a proxy of pubertal hormone exposure'.[2] The study acknowledged that the link was one of association, rather than causation, but the authors argued that a male-dominated workplace such as a financial institution perpetuates high testosterone levels which 'may perhaps eventually lead to irrational risk-taking'.[3]

Another study, in the Proceedings of the National Academy of Sciences USA, found that high testosterone levels in traders correlated with unusually successful trading days.[4] Testosterone levels were significantly higher on days when the traders beat their daily average profit. The researchers speculated that long periods of elevated testosterone, as might be the case during a market bubble, can turn risk-taking into a form of addiction, exaggerating the market's upward turn – until it deflates under the exhausting pressure of impulsivity. This physiological assessment may have some parallels with the George Soros theory of reflexivity.

So is the financial crisis solely a male affair? Not necessarily, for two reasons. First, the presence of women on trading floors may ratchet up testosterone levels among the men. And another study suggested that hormonal changes in women may also have an impact on their risk-seeking behaviour.[5] Normally, research shows that women are more risk averse than men in competitive bidding situations. But a University of Michigan study suggests that the gender gap in competitive bidding disappears during certain times of the month. 'We found that during menstruation, when levels of oestrogen are the lowest, women do not bid any differently from men.'[6] So this gender difference in bidding is driven by higher levels of sex hormones in women too. The researchers caution, however, that biology is just one factor influencing risk tolerance: education, experience, personality and cultural issues are also significant.

These studies, in themselves, are suggestive, but there is a lack of real life research on trading floors themselves, which must make one cautious in accepting these speculative interpretations. They do suggest, however, that the compliance and risk management systems in banks face an uphill struggle to discipline risk-seeking behaviour which is stimulated by sex hormones.

References

1. Is Testosterone to Blame for the Financial Crisis? Jordan Lite. 30 September 2008. www.scientificamerican.com
2. Ibid.

3. Ibid.
4. Endogenous Steroids and Financial Risk-Taking on a London Trading Floor. J. M. Coates and J. Herbert. Proceedings of the National Academy of Sciences USA 105:6167–6172. April 2008.
5. Why Can't a Woman Bid More Like a Man? Yan Chen, Peter Katuscak, Emre Ozdenoren. The Center for Economic Research and Graduate Education, Working Paper No. 275. Prague. September 2005.
6. Ibid.

AND FINALLY . . .

39

A COMBUSTIBLE MIXTURE

The main aim of this book is to present an opinionated guide to the arguments about who or what was to blame for the crisis. Where I see little merit in a case, that is perhaps obvious. In other areas the reader can make up his or her own mind. But as a brief postscript I offer my own brief synthesis of the points I consider the most important.

In a speech early in his presidency[1] Obama described the crisis as 'a perfect storm of irresponsibility and poor decision making that stretched from Wall Street to Washington to Main Street'. That seems a balanced conclusion, though more recently the political rhetoric around the world has shifted more to explanations rooted in the behaviour of the financial sector.

While not wishing to take anything away from the masters of the universe on Wall Street and in Canary Wharf, whose contribution was undoubtedly impressive, it is important to look further back in time for the roots of such a complex phenomenon.

We must begin from the observation that, for reasons not well understood by economists or anyone else, there is a business cycle. Gordon Brown's claim to have 'put an end to boom and bust' was unwise and hubristic. But why was this particular bust so dramatic and so destructive?

The principal reason may be that it came after an unusually

long upswing, which we might date back to the recovery from the crash of 1987, or perhaps even further. Over the next twenty years there were some ups and downs and miniature financial crises associated with the dot-com bubble, LTCM and the Asian troubles of the late 1990s, but they were relatively short lived. The consequences were offset by aggressive cuts in interest rates, led by the Federal Reserve, which largely succeeded in preventing those upsets from seriously damaging the real economy.

The behaviour of central banks during this period was grounded in the belief that the appropriate role for the monetary authority was to control short-term inflation in consumer prices. Inflation targeting, whether explicitly described as such, or implicit, became the core orthodoxy in central banks. The growth of credit, and the behaviour of asset prices, could be ignored and left to market forces, as long as consumer price inflation was low and stable. Inflationary conditions did remain largely benign. The monetary authorities were assisted by the arrival of new competitors in the world economy, especially China, whose competitiveness was sustained by low wage rates and a massive supplementary labour force moving from the country to the town – a new industrial revolution beginning in the late twentieth century.

Those new competitors helped to hold inflation down, by reducing the ability of Western firms to increase prices. At the same time these countries, led by China, generated large trade surpluses which they chose to invest in Western economies, particularly in the United States. That created a surplus of liquidity, holding down interest rates and reducing yields on risky assets. Low interest rates, both short and long term, allowed the build-up of leverage. Households were able to maintain their previous standard of living through borrowing, in effect from the new competitors who were holding down their wages.

So leverage built up in the system and the 'recourse to lower interest rates encouraged ever more borrowing, ever more debt accumulation and ever larger imbalances'.[2]

At the same time, deregulation in the financial sector allowed banks and some other firms to become larger and larger. They were able to acquire competitors in their core business and also to spread across other subsectors of finance, creating financial hypermarkets. These huge institutions benefited from a range of safety nets and from the famous 'Greenspan Put', which implied that the Federal Reserve would step in with lower interest rates in the event that rising asset prices, on which much financial activity was effectively based, seemed to stall.

These firms may not have explicitly thought of themselves as gambling on the basis of being 'too big to fail'. But the incentive structures within them, and the loose liquidity conditions combined with financial innovation and growing complexity, proved to be a combustible mixture. Highly diversified institutions became very difficult to manage, and size led to a species of alienation between frontline traders supported by ever more complex mathematical models, and senior managers and boards of directors. Their role should have been to constrain the traders' animal spirits, but their understanding of the dynamics of the business was limited. This mixture led to institutions which were highly vulnerable to any downturn in asset prices or tightening of financial conditions.[3]

It is relatively easy to characterize the vulnerabilities of the system as it operated in early 2007. One can also see that leverage began to expand rapidly around four years earlier. But determining the precise reasons for the timing both of this rapid expansion of leverage, and of the 2007 credit crunch, is much harder. Minsky's description of the dynamics of the process is as good as any, though one imagines even Minsky, if he were alive today, would have found it difficult to forecast that the withdrawal of support by BNP Paribas for three of its off-balance sheet vehicles would trigger a collapse on the scale we saw. When asset prices began to fall, and a liquidity squeeze started, a number of important markets collapsed like a pack of cards.

It became clear at that point that financial regulators had not been tough enough, particularly in their approach to capital reserving, to constrain risk-taking or to ensure that institutions were robust enough to cope with a period of severe stress. There are some technical explanations, which are described above, for the failures of regulation which became manifest over the last three years.

But as a former regulator (until 2003) I may attest that the political environment within which regulators worked was unfavourable to measures which tightened financial conditions, and in any event the tools regulators had at their disposal were far weaker than the interest rate weapon. The political and intellectual framework of financial regulation, until 2007 at least, was one of the belief in the power of the market, and a view that professional investors were 'consenting adults' who should be allowed to transact with each other without undue interference. The best guarantee of financial stability was that market participants had the interests of their investors and shareholders at heart, and those interests were far more powerful than any regulatory intervention.

It is also true to say that the financial sector became more powerful and more effective in the defence of its own interests. Immediately before the crisis some 40 per cent of all profits in the United States came from financial firms, giving them a huge influence, both direct and indirect, on policy makers. Also, these firms had been very successful for a long time. Who were regulators to argue that their astonishing success was built on unsound foundations? Governments were also very keen to attract mobile international financial business to their jurisdictions. Wall Street, and the City of London, were geese that laid golden eggs. They must on no account be encouraged to fly elsewhere. And whatever they may say now, there were many other countries and cities in Asia and continental Europe who would have been happy to play host to this business.

The crash has, therefore, been no end of a lesson for politicians, central bankers, regulators and financiers. A major overhaul of regulation is underway, though elements of it remain heavily contested. There is somewhat less sign of an imminent overhaul of monetary policy frameworks. In the financial sector, attitudes to risk will be influenced by the crisis for some time to come, but the experience of the past suggests that the half life of lessons from disasters is shorter than one might think, which makes it necessary to find ways of embedding these painful learnings into new laws and regulations. The comfortable belief in the self-disciplining powers of financial markets will not quickly be re-established.

References

1. Remarks on the Economy. Barack Obama. Speech at Georgetown University. 14 April 2009. www.whitehouse.gov
2. Anatomy of Crisis – the Living History of the Last Thirty Years: Economic Theory, Politics and Policy? William White. Institute of New Economic Thinking Conference. King's College, Cambridge. 9 April 2010. http://ineteconomics.org
3. The $100 Billion Question. Andrew Haldane. Speech at the Institute of Regulation & Risk North Asia. Hong Kong. 30 March 2010. www.bankofengland.co.uk

INDEX

CPSIA information can be obtained at www.ICGtesting.com
Printed in the USA
LVOW071836130513

333552LV00009B/170/P